Please help me to Keep you

06/26/04

Glad I found you.
Amber,

Love

MW00711662

READERS ADULATION for
WHY CANT YOU SEE ME?
GOOD MEN DO EXIST!

"The black man has been wronged; the black woman has been mislead. There are still good black men out here, look beyond the trees and you will find paradise. These two authors have crafted a well-written and truthful book about the African American single life. A must read if you are a single woman or man!
Anthony T. Williamson, Real-estate Investor
Sherman Oaks, CA

"This book helps men and women to realize what we don't see and what we don't want to see about ourselves, our race and our relationships. This goes beyond women, Venus, men and Mars. Young and not so young, married and unmarried can benefit from this collection of truths that Chris and Aaron have brought to our attention. ...Riveting, truthful and insightful!
Machelle Warrick-Brazile, HR Advisor
Houston, TX

"This book is a timely piece of work, which specifically addresses our issues and concerns as men and women. Chris and Aaron are giving it to us straight with no chaser! It is truly a blueprint we can dialogue from. Thank you my brothers for speaking out and telling the unabashed truth!"
Joseph Judkins, Loan Officer
Detroit, MI

"A bitter pill to swallow at times. Sistas, the blueprint has been laid out! Let's open up, no more games and choose happiness from our good men!"

Angela L. Jones, Loan Processor
Coco, FL

"A refreshing look at the age old theories facing our young black culture. Both genders should benefit from the facts dispelling some of the myths. Myths we have all been taught by the media, our families, and friends. Although this will be controversial the truths are unavoidable. We as black men have not refuted the misrepresentation of our gender. They have identified the challenges both men and women face when dating. We to often do not discuss our problems until it's too late. The vicious cycle can be broken with the acceptance of the facts presented to us in this bio of our love lives. Pure, delightful, respectable, a must read for individuals and young couples serious about taking the correct measures to communicate about black love and what it has become vs. what it can be."

Charles Starr, Sales Rep
Atlanta, GA

"A true eye opener, this book gives you insight on relationships from a black male perspective. It made me realize how women are missing out on real love. How we need each other and how important relationships should be to us both. There are still good men out there. We just need to wake up and open our eyes. In order to find true love, we must loose the baggage and meet each person that enters our life with an open mind and open heart. We must trust our instincts to make the right choices in order to have a fulfilling, trusting, and lasting relationship. Stop loving yourself and give someone the chance to love you. May the reading and applying of the information in the book, bring about a change and healing for African American relationships."

Tara King, Administrative Assistant
Asbury Park, NJ

First Printing 2003

Editing by Schkira Shareef

Cover Design by Vita Rome

Love Life Publishing, LLC
175 W Wieuca Rd NE
Suite 211
Atlanta GA, 30342
(877) 289-5220

Library of Congress Catalog Card No: 2003098428
ISBN 0-9747496-0-5

Printed in the United States of America

In loving memory of

To my mentor, L. Mark Daniels, who set my life on the right path in high school. Without your guidance, I would probably not be alive. Thank you to his family for sharing him with those of us whom would not have made it without him.

Chris Cokley

This book is dedicated with affection and deepest love to my grandmother, Gladys Grier. Your wisdom, support, strength, and love have been the backbone of my existence. I'll never forget the countless lessons you've taught me. I miss you.

Aaron Blake

Special thanks for giving us life

To my mother, Alma Cokley, I love you. Thank you for your support and guidance. You have been the inspiration for whom I have become. Mom, you are my example of strength and character. Watching you raise four children, without ever complaining about the lack of emotional or financial support from our fathers. Taught me more about life than any words I've ever read or heard. Not only did you go back to school as an adult and transition from housewife to licensed nurse; you inspired all four of your children to experience higher education. I know, by the way you look at me that you're proud of me. I only hope that you can see how proud I am of you. Your love is food for my soul.

Chris Cokley

To my adoring mother, Deborah Blake Day words could never describe the depth of the love I feel for you. You deserve endless thanks for guidance support, love, advice and sacrifice. I thank you for supplying me with the hopes, dreams and inspirations that shaped the man I am today. Mom now that I am an adult with children of my own. I realize how much dedication it took on your part to raise a family alone. I also know that it must have been hard to sit back and watch someone you loved so much, make so many mistakes. However, you did and were always there to welcome me with open mind, open heart and open arms. I am so proud to have such a wonderful woman to call my mother. I Love You

Aaron Blake

CONTENT

I. ORIGIN OF A GOOD MAN

II. THROUGH THE EYES OF GOOD MEN

III. WHAT MEN WANT AND WOMEN NEED

IV. WILL YOU MARRY ME?

ACKNOWLEDGEMENTS

I, Chris Cokley, would like to say writing this book was a personally tormenting ordeal. Although my heart has been in the right place, I have not succeeded at building a strong family yet. And I realize that I never will, if we don't start to have serious dialog about love, commitment, and marriage in our community.

Let me start with the loving memory of my grandmothers Hattie Cokley, dedicated wife and mother. Lila Pearl Carter, wife, mother of eight children and entrepreneur, your examples were priceless in my development. Thank you, Liza for your support, I pray that you get everything you seek in life. Thank you to my sisters, Wanda and Brita, who've always encouraged me. To my four beautiful nieces, Nicole, Kera, Chaniquah, and Quasheea, find true love and everything else will follow. To my brother Marvin, thank you for pushing me to excel at everything.

Very special thanks to Leslie Greene of **Raising the Standard Entertainment, Inc.** for your help in launching this project. Many thanks to my best friend and co-author, Aaron Blake, who pushed for us to write this book. Love is around the corner for you. To the women I chose to share my life with, our experiences have colored the content of the book. Everything happens for a reason. Perhaps this book is the reason we met; to grow and prepare for love. In doing so, we might also help someone else to love again.

Aaron Blake:

In a project that has taken a lifetime to birth, it is impossible to thank the many people who have loved, supported and inspired me to write this book. However, I would like to thank my beautiful daughters, Amanda and Aviance, You are truly my inspiration and I love you very much. My ex-wife, Niecie, Thank you for your patience and understanding. My lovely sisters, Anissa and Ahdina, thanks for being there to take care of Mommy while your big brother set off to make his way in the world. I love you more than words can say. My sister Toi, thanks for all the fun memories. My brother Daryl, I love you Bro. My father, Earnest Daniel, I love you. My homegirl, Nancy, thanks for always lending your ear when I needed it. My cousin, Eryk, your father would be so happy at how close we've become. Thanks for your endless support. To Nequila, I'll always cherish the times we shared.

Special thanks, and tremendous gratitude to my main man, Neal. Thanks for always being there for me no matter what and thanks for being a positive example of a married, responsible Black man. Thank you, Maggie Moore, my Uncle Rodney, Rodney Day, and the whole Jackson family, especially Les Jackson. To my Uncle Murphy and my grandfather Hector Blake I love you. Rest in peace. Last, but certainly not least, I would like to thank Chris Cokley, you are my family, my best friend. I couldn't imagine my life without you in it. I love you, Bro.

INTRODUCTION

Somewhere, somehow, over the course of our lives, we've forgotten what it was like to be with each other. Black love has lost its sense of direction and purpose. We've changed our beliefs, our values, and along the way lost our capacity for unconditional love for one another. We go through each day knowing in our hearts that something isn't right, but also not knowing how to fix what's wrong. We're like dogs chasing our tails around in circles. We search for new ways to fill the void, but at the end of each day the feeling of emptiness returns bigger and stronger than ever. We start to wonder if we'll ever get this love thing right.

This book is a plea, an attempt to get you to understand what good black men are experiencing so we can have meaningful interactions with black women. Only with understanding can we love and support each other more completely.

Let's not wait for something magical to happen. It's up to us to mend the differences, which exist between us. We've been involved in countless conversations about what's wrong with Black Love and have read numerous books and articles on the subject. However, We've felt like something was missing. Nobody was saying what really needed to be said.

The book is not a declaration of blame, but merely an instrument to point out some specifics you may not have thought about, what you can't see, or maybe have turned a deaf ear to. We are not going to tell you what to do to make the bad men you have met better. We are asking the good women to stop dating bad men in hopes of changing them. And, we are asking good men to stop dating the wrong women just because they look good. Take the time to find each other and give true love and family a chance to survive and flourish. We must stand together and introduce the rebirth of Black Love.

We don't have degrees that qualify us to talk to you about love and relationships. All we have are experiences as men who have always wanted to be married with children. Now, we find ourselves in our mid-thirties, both unmarried and one childless. As we look back on the reason why and talk to other men who feel the way we do, this book details what we found.

I never imagined that I would write a book or voice my opinions to anyone other than my close group of friends. They came to look forward to my responses to the most commonly asked questions about dating and would reply that I should do seminars on dating. But what inspires me more than anything is a personal mission statement to assist African American families in becoming financially independent. As a result, I have spent the last sixteen years teaching families about how money works and how to properly prepare for all their financial needs. In so doing, the drastic disappearance of the African American family is painfully obvious. Now, how can I help families if we don't have any left?

In lieu of this reality, my co-author mentioned that we should do more. According to Aaron, "We should be doing more I don't know what we should be doing but I feel like we have not found our calling." After much contemplation, we decided to expand our crusade to include the rebuilding of the African American family. With a strong nucleus in place, we can then teach them how to become financially independent.

I've often said that no one betrays us like us. Well, nobody's going to help us either but us. I want to resolve the challenges that keep us away from one another. Moreover, I want to say what good men have wanted to say for a long time now. " Why Can't You See Me? Good Men Do Exist!"

"I Apologize, I'm Sorry, please forgive me. I'm sorry that I make it so difficult for you to communicate with me sometimes and I don't always show you how I really feel about you. I don't mean to make it so hard for you to love me."

I APOLOGIZE

Every man messes up sometimes, despite the best intentions. Our fragile egos, our imperfections, our weaknesses, and our shortcomings are what make us human. By virtue of being human, there will be times, now and in the future, when we will let you down, make you angry, disappoint you, shock you and manipulate you. We will attempt to control you, be insensitive to your needs, be dishonest and lose our tempers. We're not perfect and neither are you. Together we won't be perfect either. However, we're all we have. Now, I don't proclaim to be the spokesperson for the entire male race, but someone has to be man enough to say it, so I will. "I Apologize, I'm Sorry, please forgive me." I'm sorry that I make it so difficult for you to communicate with me sometimes and I don't always show you how I really feel about you. I don't mean to make it so hard for you to love me. I'm sorry, please forgive me. I apologize for not praising you enough and treating you like the queen you are. I'm sorry that I was so thoughtless and didn't thank you everyday for raising our children. Please forgive me. I'm truly sorry. I apologize for not always being there when you needed me and for not letting you know how much I have always needed you. Forgive me for being so thoughtless, cruel and stubborn. I'm so sorry for not telling you every second, of every minute, of every hour that you are a very important part of my life. Please forgive me for criticizing you when I know you only wanted to help, for not being committed when I knew you were, for neglecting you when all you wanted to do was love me. I'm sorry, I really am sorry. I apologize for being irresponsible and immature, for letting you work two jobs and I wouldn't look for one. I'm sorry that I called you out of your name. Please forgive me. I'm sorry that I wasn't a better son, a better boyfriend, a better husband, and better man. Please forgive me for not having all the answers to your questions. I'm sorry I made you cry. I'm sorry I lied to you. I'm sorry that you hungered for accomplishment and all I did was put you down. I'm sorry I yelled at you and smacked you around. I'm sorry I made you afraid of me when I was supposed to be the one protecting you. Will you please forgive me? I'm sorry for leaving you all alone to raise our children, for not paying child support, for breaking up our homes, for leaving you. I apologize for not being a better teacher and for not leading our family spiritually. Please forgive me. I'm sorry I feared intimacy and I never let you in. I'm sorry for influencing you with material seduction, for not living up to my potential, for not having any ambition. I apologize for being addicted to Playstation2 instead of being addicted to you. I'm sorry, please forgive me. I apologize for my lack of sexual integrity, premature ejaculations, and while making love to you, only thinking of myself. I apologize for sleeping around with other women endangering your health. I'm sorry for being financially irresponsible, undependable and a procrastinator. I also apologize for all the things I've failed to mention in this apology. I'm sorry for not telling you you're sexy, you're special and you're beautiful. Forgive me for not saying, I like you, I want you, I need you, I love you. Thank you for choosing to read my words. I hope you received the love within them. Once again, I apologize, please forgive me, I'm sorry.

"Bad men have pretended to be good men for so long, what do good men have to be to get you to see we exist!"

The Good Man

Sometimes I cry when I see the tears that men have brought to your eyes.
When he lies little does he know that black love is what dies.
Because your ability to trust any man starts to subside.
When he cheats he doubles his impact because there are two women affected by his deceit.
And no longer will you be able to let your vulnerability shine through.
So now when you meet a good man what are you to do.
When he won't commit making your relationship, and in some cases your children illicit.
And your left trying to decide should you stay or should you split.
Only to start all over and possibly go thru the same shit makes you want to just quit.
That's another piece of black love that no longer exists.

Sometimes I cry when I see women trade their bodies for material gain.
Believing that emotional treasure is a myth that if she continues to chase it she will go insane.
So to preserve her heart and mind she decides she must play the game and walk the line.
That she must lie, cheat, and master the art of deceit
To heal her heartache as she looses at love and suffer what appears to be endless defeat.
That if she does to men what has been done to her that somehow she would seek revenge.
But in the end the only hearts she breaks is that of good men.

Men who want to give her more just to find out that she has decided to be a whore.
Oh, I know you're not a whore you just date
But before or after you have sex make no mistake
Dinner, movies, and expensive gifts, must be on your plate
Or part of the plan, pay a few bills will move him closer to being your man.

Sometimes I cry when I sit back and reflect
On all the hurt and damaged women I have met. That no matter how hard I tried to love them and fill their life with bliss
Only to find they could not love me back they did not believe I exist.
A man that wants a wife, and would love a child,
A man that knows how to treat a woman and adore her smiles.
He appreciates her worth and would gladly provide for her the rest of her days on this earth.
A man that would work all day and make love to her all night,
Help the kids with their homework and break up their fights.
A man that knows were he is going and has a plan of how to get there
But knows success is empty without someone with whom to share.

Today I want to cry, but instead I ask why
Do you ask for a good man if you don't believe he exists?
If you meet him your going to treat him like he probably ain't shit.
You're looking around trying to find his flaws and add him to the dog list

When the problem is that in your mind this man is just a myth.

He cannot be your lover only a friend, that way he is close but can't get in.

In your heart you refuse to be a loving host because in your mind this man must be a ghost.

A good man needs trust, respect, love, and peace of mind.

A woman that will put it all on the line for a chance to make him hers for all time.

But you no longer have these things to give to a brother

Because you gave it to another that bad man pretending to be good.... that undercover brother.

The one who will lie, cheat, run from commitment and fill your world with deceit and resentment. Making it impossible for you to recognize a good man even if God sent him.

If you're not ready to love then you should not date because all this confusion is turning black love into black hate.

By Chris Cokley

"Most men by their twenties are consciously or unconsciously carrying the hurt and pain of teenage relationships that did not last. This haunts them today and is probably the most powerful force in what type of men they are in relationships."

I. ORIGIN OF A GOOD MAN

Some say that good or bad men are a result of what their parents did or didn't do. Also, whether they had a father figure in their life to teach them how to be a man. All these factors may play a small role in the type of man that a young boy grows up to be. But I believe the most powerful factors in the development of a man are the women he has encountered.

Chronology of Dating

We start this book with a depiction of the beginning of male and female interaction. We believe and will attempt to prove it is the foundation of male development. There was a time when boys were groomed for marriage by their fathers and girls by their mothers. Their marriages were arranged and no dating was necessary because the people who raised them were the people who chose their mates.

Arranged marriages were a vital part of tradition and rearing. Matrimony was arranged to maximize compatibility between participants. Secondly, it was to ensure the strength and longevity of families. Furthermore, the new union would serve as a positive reflection on the community. Although this process did not involve love, it was effective because it ensured that factors such as culture, religion, environment, and family approval would provide a strong foundation. I think that anyone that has experienced a relationship would agree that love could grow in the right foundation. I also think most would agree that without a strong foundation, love is not enough.

Once picking your mate became your own responsibility and the process of dating or courtship was developed, it began to change the development of black men. Why, you ask? Well, African Americans really have no culture. We are a mix of many different cultures. We love German cars, Italian suits, Chinese food, multi-cultural music and movies. We are members of many different religions such as Christian, Muslim, or Jewish, just to name a few. And of course, there are sects in each of the religions. Our many backgrounds come from all over America, and in some cases the world. Subsequently, the environments in which we were raised are very different in some cases. And of course, economic status had an affect on that environment.

As we ventured out to determine who we are and what we want out of life as individuals, we tended to move farther and farther away from our families. More and more as the years passed, it made family approval and support non-existent in a lot of relationships.

So, how do most black men decide who they are going to be in today's society? The answer is based on what women want or what's popular. I know this is contrary to popular belief, but I believe how a boy develops into a man has a little to do with his parents' relationship and whether his father or mother was in the household. I believe a larger percentage of true development into manhood comes from interaction with women. Since there never has been and probably never will be a totally accurate rule book on dating that works for everyone and there is no guideline in the word of God, men will forever be baffled and confused by the process.

Women always ask, why do men lie so much? Well, here is the most popular answer. Most men are so confused by what women want and how to date. Men have come up with the philosophy of telling women whatever they want to hear. This gets women to like them and be intimate with them so they can cut through the bullshit of dating. You see, most men hate dating with a passion, and only do it because most women require it as a way to prove men are interested in more than just sex. Most men want to get to the sex as fast as possible, hoping that the stress of dating and lying will go away and the true intention for the relationship can be revealed.

Women got into the habit of telling men lies when first meeting them like, "I'm not looking for a serious relationship," in hopes of not scaring men off. Hoping that once he got to know her, he would decide that she was the one for him. When he didn't, she would get mad at him. What usually happens is that the stress intensifies because the woman feels like she has given you a part of her based on the lies and now you owe her a part of you.

The truth is that sex is not a prize or a tool for negotiation. You exchanged a part of each other, when you choose to engage in intercourse. Most women are not honest about what they want in a man, mainly because they don't know what they want. Most men don't know what they should be to make a woman happy, so they lie until they figure out what she wants and whether they are capable of being what she wants. If they are not comfortable being what she is looking for, they move on to the next girl until they find one with which they are comfortable. So, before I go any further, let's go back to the beginning.

I guess boys and girls began to cross each other's path early in life and we didn't seem to be on the same page from the beginning. Girls being more advanced physically and mentally than boys their age began to like boys at a young age. They would start to talk about boys to their girlfriends and would have their first crush on the boy next door. This takes place at a time when boys still think girl just get in the way of them playing. When boys began to really like girls they fell hard, and the affection of women would become the motivation for everything they do in life. By their teenage years, girls have begun to develop taste and now are attracted to the popular guys only, the athletes and entertainers, good-looking boys with good hair, or smart boys. Now, this began the creation of two types of men: the lover and the hustler.

The lover is the guy who got all the attention from multiple girls, because he was popular, attractive, or smart. He watched girls compete for his attention and when he would get caught with different girls, they would get mad at each other and forgive him. He achieved the most powerful emotion his heart could imagine, love from a girl with little to know effort. For that, a large percentage of this type of man would learn to never appreciate love or respect it. Consequently, he never appreciates anything or anyone. Others would eventually learn to respect and appreciate love much later in life.

The hustler had the opposite happen. He realized early in life that to achieve the love of a girl, he would have to become popular and begin to look for ways to achieve that. Some began to work out to look better, others began to play sports and practice hard to be the best, and to study hard to get good grades. But soon they discovered that money was the great equalizer to talent or good looks. Money could lead to Power, which could lead to Fame. If you had one of the three or all three, the girls would love you. Depending on how long it took him to become successful and how many times he was hurt and rejected by women along the way that determined what type of man he would become.

This all began in middle and high school between the ages of 12 and 15. Parents did not help during this period of time, because they did not realize how much this would shape the psychology of their children as it relates to dating and finding a mate. Instead, they added to the confusion in an attempt to keep their children from becoming sexually active too young. They taught their little girls to stay focused on school so they would always be able to take care of themselves. Don't ever depend on a man. Get established on your own and don't trust boys. They just want one thing and they will leave you pregnant and alone. So no matter what he says keep your legs closed and say no until you're married.

Most girls would listen to part of this advice. They would not leave the boys alone. They would stay focused on school and prepare themselves to make it in life on their own terms, with or without a man. The unfortunate truth is that a lot of girls got permanently sidetracked because they did get pregnant. This may have resulted in them never finishing school, and possibly changing all their goals. Many however, would persevere even through single parenthood to achieve their goals.

Now boys were encouraged by both parents to be popular. It was considered cute and parents would react with pride if girls were attracted to him. If he did not have a talent that was visible early in life, like sports or really good grades, then the hope was that he would at least graduate from high school, go to college, or at the very least move out the house and get a job. But very few boys were told anything about girls or sex.

The beauty and the pain of high school were that you had to start all over again. Some of the popular people in middle school continued their reign in high school and some that were invisible in middle school remained invisible in high school. Then there were those that learned the game and changed their positions in life and joined the popular ranks. For some it happened naturally because they grew into their looks and were physically attractive. Others worked at it and became star athletes, entertainers, and leaders. Another group used money and cars, most of which came from their parents. The stakes were higher now because elements like sex and pregnancy gave new meaning to the word love for teenagers. At this point, the dynamics of dating began to become even more complex, because the popular guys would take advantage of the not so popular girls at their school and the popular girls from other schools. And the popular girl would date popular guys from neighboring schools or college men. This left a large number of young boys who got very little to no love at all.

During this period of time is when a lot of heartbreak and disappointment happens and gives birth to some of the mindsets that have kept black men and women apart for decades. If a boy found a girlfriend in high school, he thought he found his wife and would fall deeply in love with her. This would most likely become the biggest heartbreak of his life.

For example:

My name is Calvin. I met Mia when I was sixteen and leaving for college. We dated for a year while I was in college and she stayed home to finish her last year of high school. She would visit me from time to time and I thought I had found my wife. I saved every dime I made from working while I was in college and bought her a ring that I intended to give to her over the holiday break.

When I got home and went to visit her at her parent's house, everyone looked so sad. Her parents demanded that she tell me, so she did. She proceeded to explain to me that she was pregnant but not by me, by the boy who lived next door to her. He was her boyfriend through childhood and they had a few more sexual encounters while I was away at college. When I returned home to my family they could see on my face that something terrible had happened. They all thought that I had asked her to marry me and she said no. But the story was a lot worse.

I did not fall in love again for over five years. Although I dated many beautiful women, I would not commit to any of them. I went on to date as many as four or five women at a time. I let go and began to realize that what goes around comes around.

After returning to my hometown, I saw Mia at a local club. She was still living at home with her parents raising her child as a single parent mom. You see, Mia was a teenage model and one of the prettiest women I had ever seen. Now look at her. I believed her life was messed up because of what she did to me, and I began to think about what my life was going to be like if I did not stop dating all these women with out making a commitment.

On the other hand, a woman being wiser and better counseled knew that if she decided to have a boyfriend early in life, he would probably not be her husband. Although she may be hurt when they broke up, she bounces back and moves on with little lasting emotional damage. You see, men are far more sensitive in their teenage years than women. Women would not suffer lasting emotional damage until the relationships they would have in their twenties.

Most men by their twenties are consciously or unconsciously carrying the hurt and pain of teenage relationships that did not last. This haunts them today and is probably the most powerful force in what type of man they are in relationships.

Now when high school ended and it was time to decide what to do with your life, most of our decisions were determined by our high school experience. Most athletes went to college for another chance to be a star and continue the good life. Those athletes whose grades were not good enough joined the military to play sports and women love men in uniform. Some stayed home with mom where they were guaranteed her love no matter what. Then you had the hustler who was determined to change his status to gain the love of a woman. As a result, some went to college and others hit the streets.

While most men have no real idea of how they are going to impress women, some became hustlers on the street because they could see fast money, and nice cars attracted pretty women to that type of man. A small few became entrepreneurs and started their own businesses or took over a family business.

In college, our views and goals in the area of relationships really started to take form. The lovers continued to get together with as many women as they could get their hands on. But things changed a little because college had more avenues for boys to become popular like fraternities, student organizations, many more sports, arts, and theater. It appears that most black men and women were on the same page in college. Everybody was dating but nobody wanted to commit to a long-term relationship.

There were a small few who truly looked for and found their spouses in college. Most other cultures see college as the perfect time to find their potential spouses and far more of them do and marry right out of college. But most of us believed that we were too young and had not found ourselves enough to make a decision to be committed to one person for life. Many women and men have said these lines: I'm too young to get married. I'm focusing on my career first. I have to prove that I could be successful on my own before I get married. I plan to start my career and live on my own for a while before I get married. Everything became about career for a lot of women and a small group of men. The rest partied until they ran out of time and money and had to leave college to get a job.

Now the whole game changed because the incubator that we called college was over. In college, you really did not need a lot of money or a nice car. We all lived in dorms or apartments with roommates. So personality, popularity, and good looks went a long way on campus. But as adults we were now being judged by our success. Women look at the homes men live in and the cars they drive and how much money they have to take them out on dates. So as you can see, boys develop into certain types of men with women in mind every step of the way. Since it is clear to men that money is a very important quality women want, getting money is the focus of most young men.

God Created Man, Women Define Him

Understand that men are not thoughtless creatures. Everything that we do we do for a reason and that reason is women. Women are always the single most important driving force behind all our behavior. The way we dress, our jobs, cars, homes, are all to gain a women's approval. By this time you've begun to see where I'm going in explaining the type of men who were produced from the dating scene in middle, high school and college. Clearly, men reacted to what women wanted from the beginning.

I could go back even further to just the relationship that most little boys have with their mothers, but I don't think that had as big an effect as dating did on what type of men they become in relationships. I bet a lot of women are saying right now that we are trying to blame our shortcomings on them. I believe that there are a small percentage of men that have made conscious decisions to create lives full of substance and depth despite the experiences they have had with women. I would like to consider myself that type of man, a product of education, observation, and self-improvement. As a man of great substance and depth on many issues, I have to admit that I had the freedom to develop intellectually because I never had to chase women. I also had very wealthy and powerful mentors in my life that taught me the most important thing I could do is to be a leader. Also, if you want people to follow you, they must feel like you have something to offer so I focused on getting better everyday. To do this successfully, I had to change from the desire to impress women to the desire to lead one, so I got married at 23 years old.

I have spent 95% of my adult life in relationships with some of the most interesting and sensual women I've had the pleasure to meet. Most of my relationships were a result of women who expressed an interest in getting to know me. Or, a third party thought we should meet so they set us up on a date. I can count on one hand how many women I've approached as a total stranger and introduced myself for the purpose of dating them. I was blessed with enough charisma to attract great people in my life, especially the opposite sex. I include that not to lay blame on women for our shortcomings, but to make women aware of how influential they are in our lives. As an example, what plenty of good women previously denounced as shortcomings, such as criminal records or illegal careers have become socially acceptable to most women today.

You see, women of the baby boomer generation and a large part of Generation X went off to pursue their careers, leaving the men behind with excuses like, "I don't have time for a relationship" or "I'm focusing on my career" or "I'm not ready to settle down." They left our men looking for love from all the wrong women and handed the power to generation Y (those born after 1970 or the middle of the Hip-Hop culture); to dictate what women wanted from men. They changed everything that we learned earlier in life, for instance. When I was graduating from high school, I knew that if I went to college I would be more attractive to women and if I went to jail, certain women would never date me again. Generation Y came along and said if I go to college I'm probably square and a nice guy. Furthermore, most women would not date me. But if I go to jail, I'm probably a thug, a gangster, or a bad boy and all the girls will love me.

When I was growing up, nobody admitted to being drug dealers. Men did everything they could to hide their illegal business from women because no woman would date a drug dealer. And of course, her parents would die! Now, women of Generation Y only date drug dealers because they spend the most money on them and men brag on TV about their illegal past. In the past, if you were intelligent and could articulate your thoughts, women would fall in love with you. Now you can speak slang, most people don't understand what you're saying and women love you. I did not get a car until I was a senior in college, but I had girlfriends the entire time. Currently, if you don't have a nice car sitting on 20" rims, you can't get a pretty girlfriend. The bottom line is that women got so caught up in the illegal, fast money and the bad boy image of the Hip-Hop culture that nobody thought of the affects it would have on the African American culture as a whole.

The Myth about Men in America

As Black people living in America, we are in serious economic trouble. In every problem that this country faces we are leading the way. We have the highest rate of unemployment, the fastest growing female AIDS cases, the worst healthcare plans, (if we have any at all). We have the highest percentage of our population of males in prison, the least amount invested for retirement, we save very little money for the education of our children, etc... The list is endless.

We could actually write a book on the state of our culture or lack thereof, in itself. The absence of the Black male in most households contributes greatly to all those problems. Why is the Black man absent from the household? Well we are lead to believe it's by choice, but those who are in power can manipulate choice. It's like a multiple-choice exam, you're given four possible choices and you must pick one of the four to be considered correct by who ever created the exam. The laws, media, corporations, and women, have all come up with a set of choices for men to make that contradict each other and what's required for black men to survive mentally, physically and financially. And if the black man fails, so do the black family and the community. This is why black men and women must wake up and realize that they do not have to choose from what is presented to them and dare to go against the system. We must stop the brainwashing and traditions of bad choices and self-destructive behavior among black men and women. Maybe we should choose entrepreneurship vs. employment, marriage vs. single, investments vs. savings, frugality vs. flamboyance, protection vs. disease, family vs. children, love vs. hate, courage vs. fear etc... First we must destroy the myths; here are the top ten responses that women gave as to why men are not in the home and a reply from the men.

10 MYTHS ABOUT MEN

1. **They are all dogs** - some men do share similar living arrangements as dogs, meaning that someone may be taking care of them and therefore they may share some of the characteristics such as playful, dependent and constantly crave attention. Like dogs, many men are not in control of their lives. A lot of men don't make enough money to support themselves, let alone a family. Therefore, they can't commit to provide for someone else. This feeling of confinement that dependency causes, increases men's desire for intimacy, so they look for women who will accept their situation or they lie about it. What you need to do is find a man who is financially responsible, and looking for a commitment and you may have a loyal dog instead of a straying dog. Dogs that have control and live free in the wild actually have most of the characteristics you would kill to find in a man such as loyal,

smart, and tenacious. He does everything his family or pack needs instinctively.

2. **They can't be trusted** – Men can be trusted in good relationships. The key is to focus on having a fulfilling relationship. Studies have proven that neither men nor women can be trusted when they are unhappy.

3. **They only want one thing sex** – Men want to be happy just like women do. Unfortunately, sex is one of the few things that make men happy with women all the time. Some times it seems like sex is the only time we're happy at all, because we don't check to make sure we're compatible with each other. If a man realizes that you're fun to be around, he will focus on more than sex. Most women aren't fun anymore; they're too busy trying to make sure nobody takes advantage of them.

4. **They value your body more than your mind** - Instinctively men look for women who can meet their physical and emotional needs. Their intellectual needs are supposed to be met by the word of God and higher education Subsequently, they are supposed to pass this knowledge on to their wives. Obviously, society has changed, but unfortunately only the most intellectual men changed with it. Intellect will always be third to his physical and emotional needs. Even to an intellectual man who can appreciate your mind.

5. **They enjoy being single** – Men don't enjoy being single. They just hate to be hurt. If a man could get a guarantee that the next woman he fell in love with would make him happy for the rest of his life, all men would sign up for that. You see men are more afraid of being hurt than women. The only way to avoid being hurt is to avoid falling in love, and the only way to avoid falling in love is to avoid giving one woman your undivided attention. Love cannot be controlled; it can only be avoided.

6. **They are intimidated by how much money women make** – History has proven that he who has the money has the power. It may be conscious or unconscious, but most women who make more money will not love nor submit to a man unconditionally. Eventually his manhood is called into question if he is not capable of providing a better lifestyle for her than she can provide for herself. So to avoid drama, some men will avoid women who wear their careers like a banner.

7. **They don't respect women** – A real man respects a woman even if she does not respect herself. What is disrespectful and what is gangster or bad boy confuse so many brothers. Women seem to love a bad boy although; his actions are clearly disrespectful most of the time. Disrespect seems to be based on who is doing it. If the man is famous, attractive, or wealthy he can get away with it. I witnessed a brother leaning

on a new Mercedes S500 with three very attractive women standing in front of him. He proceeded to talk about the size of their asses for 15 minutes while they stood there and giggled. Now had I approached these same women without a sign of wealth or money, how long do you think they would have let me talk to them about their asses? Not at all! Women must reclaim their respect.

8. **They won't grow up** – Responsibility accelerates maturity. Most black men are not given a lot of responsibility. Some of them are allowed to stay home with their mothers well into their twenties, and in some cases, their thirties. Look for a responsible man, don't try to create one. And as long as he handles his responsibility, you both can enjoy life like big kids if you want.

9. **They are afraid of love** – As I said before, men are not afraid of love, just deathly afraid of being hurt. All men can love again with the right women. You must make sure you're the right women.

10. **They are afraid of commitment** – Some men can love you but won't commit. Well, commitment requires belief in the relationship and a relationship has many facets. You must have them all going great; things like love, trust, communication, passion, etc., to get a good man to commit.

I want to scream every time I hear a relationship discussion on the radio or television. We always hear the question, "What do women need a man for?" And then we hear statements like, "Why don't women consider dating men who make less money? All the successful black women out there intimidate men. There are not enough brothers who have their act together. Men don't want to commit and that all men cheat and lie! Women make all the money so they are calling all the shots!" I agree that women do call all the shots, but it is not because they make all the money.

Based on information I found from The Bureau of Labor Statistics and The Bureau of the Census revised March 2002, I can't understand why black men are portrayed as the problem. Let us review some of the numbers together. These statistics are based on African Americans age 25, and older and any multi-racial persons including African American as one of the two races they claim. There are 8,931,000 males and 11,428,000 females in the US. That's 2,497,000 more women than men. The amount of men that go to college is 37% to 40.7% of women a 3.7% difference. 12.5% of men graduate with a bachelors degree, or higher to 13.9% of women that graduate a 1.4% difference. Yet, in higher education women account for 501,000 masters degree holders while men account for 294,000 masters degree holders. Because of this statistic, it is always said that black women are doing so much better than their male counterparts. But what is not mentioned is the fact that most women obtain their masters degree in areas like sociology and psychology, which pay less than fields like engineering and finance, for example. This is where most men hold their masters degrees. For this reason, black men with masters degrees earn on average 8,000 dollars more a year than their female counterparts.

Also, men account for 65,000 of the doctorate degree holders to 44,000 women doctorate degree holders. As you can see, men are not that far behind in education. Let's see if the numbers support that theory. There are 1,460,000 men to 2,000,000 women who graduated from college. That's 86% or 1,255,000 college educated men and 84.4% or 1,694,000 college educated women earning income at the time of this statistical data. Obviously, there are more women with degrees in the workforce. This is not because men have fallen so far behind, but because there's just more women than men.

Now let's examine income in the African American community. With this we can put an end to all the negative talk about black men not taking care of their business. The average income of college-educated men is $43,274 as opposed to college-educated women at $36,463. As a matter of fact, more men earn more money than women in every income category except two. To be more specific, 5,164,000 women live in poverty in this country as opposed to 3,261,000 men. That is, poverty meaning no income. Also, 2,774,000 women and 1,847,000 men earn

$10,000 to $24,999 a year, while 1,607,000 women and 1,368,000 men earn $25,000 to $34,999 a year. You see we have both the largest African American upper class and the largest African American lower class in our history. The problem is how do you define middle class? It almost doesn't seem fair to say that someone earning $15,000 to $25,000 in any major metropolitan area is middle class. Yet most statistical data does giving us the perception that we are doing better financially than we are.

Now as the income increases so do the number of men dominating the categories. For example, 1,286,000 men and 1,173,000 women earn $35,000 to $49,999 a year, while 807,000 men and 547,000 women earn $50,000 to $74,999 a year. Let's pursue this even further. 222,000 men and 96,000 women earn $75,000 to $99,999 a year, while 142,000 men and 68,000 women earn $100,000 a year and over. That's 573,000 more men earning more than women in the bracket of $35,000 and up. Let's face it, this is the income bracket that counts because very few people are living a great lifestyle at less than $35,000 of income. Please stop saying that women are doing it and men need to get their act together because it's simply not true. Not because we said so, but because that is what statistics show. What is happening is that all good men are not driving flashy cars and living in huge homes. They refuse to invest their hard-earned money on dating women who don't know what they really want or know how to get it. A good man would much rather invest in the stock market. And now, they are starting to date over the Internet, date outside our race and looking at mail order brides from other countries.

To prove my point, I have a co-worker who is a successful black male and owns his home. He went on vacation and when he returned he gave me the vacation tape to watch. As I watched the tape I realized the vacation was set up for men looking to marry women from another country. And there were quite a few black men on the tape looking for brides. A few months later he brought his new wife to the office to meet us. She barely spoke English so he was teaching her and she was teaching him Spanish. She was very attractive and he said to me that her friends and relatives wanted to know if he had any friends who want to get married. While we're on the subject, let's put to rest the rumor that men don't commit.

Let's look at some more statistics. According to statistical data, out of 9,944,000 men 18 and older, 4,896,000 got married and 4,234,000 still live with their spouses. Out of 12,414,000 women 18 and older 4,693,000 were married and only 3,750,000 still lived with their spouse. Also, 1,661,000 women were divorced and 882,000 men were divorced. Now you can read into this data a lot of ways. First 49% of black men get married, while only 37% of women get married. Despite the fact that there are 2,470,000 more women than men, 203,000 more men got married. I imagine that some of you are asking how could the numbers be so different? Looking at the above statistic, take into consideration that some men and women marry outside of their race. The point is that Black men commit to marriage more than black women do. Now, to whom they marry and why is part of what we intend to discuss in this book.

The myth that says sisters are doing so well and that they don't need us anymore has created a false sense of female security. The truth is that if we don't find our way back to each other soon, the repercussions will be ten times worse than they are today. Looking at this last statistic, 39% of single African Americans live below the poverty line while only 6.1% of married African Americans live in poverty. This clearly states that we do much better together than we do apart, not to mention what a difference it would make in our children.

The moral of this story is there are as many good black men making enough money to support a family, as there are black women. The problem is women of all income levels are trying to date the 1,171,000 men who earn over $50,000 a year, and not for the right reasons. Most women don't just want a man working or a man making a little more than they do. They want a man doing a lot better than them. Women with no income are going after the top income earners not to find a husband but to get his money. Not many women want to find a husband with whom to work and build a better life together. Now, women want men who can change their lives financially, instantly and all they believe they need to bring to the table is sex. When the demand from women for a better life is instant, men will try to fill the demand instantly. This may be part of the reason we have so many black men in jail, from selling drugs or robbery. They are simply trying to get fast money to satisfy their mother, baby's mother, girlfriend, or just trying to impress women in general. We believe there are millions of good women who would lock arms with a good man and build a beautiful life together. The problem is the women don't believe good men exist and the men don't believe women care about anything but money.

"Most women of other cultures are still very traditional when it comes to dating. They want flowers, cards, dinner, and time with their boyfriend with one goal in mind to get married. If they have a financial problem, they call their fathers not their boyfriends."

Men and the Race Card

Since more than 50% of black women live below the poverty line, money and a better quality of life are driving forces in dating. Quite frankly, most don't care what or who they have to do as long as he's got money. This is a major reason why most men distrust black women more and more each day, thus sending them looking at women of other ethnicities. I hear people ask why are so many successful black men marrying white women or women of other cultures? I think the answer is simple. Black men do want to commit and get married but they would like to believe it is for love, not money.

Black women, like the men suffer from material deprivation. Therefore, when they get money or a man with money, they want to spend as much of it as they can on material things. A lot of black women feel they need and deserve material things. If you're going to be their man you should buy these things for them and pay their bills. They want everything while dating because very few believe in love and marriage anymore. Of course, this mentality causes drama with good men looking for financially responsible women who will respect how hard they had to work to make their money. If you observe most other cultures, you find very few poor or middle class women who care about diamonds, furs, designer bags, and designer shoes like black women. Most women of other cultures are still very traditional when it comes to dating. They want flowers, cards, dinner, and time with their boyfriend, with one goal in mind to get married. If they have a financial problem, they call their fathers not their boyfriends. They give more than they get putting their man first in their lives. Some of these women are chastised or disowned by their families for deciding to date outside their race. Their man becomes all they have to depend on for emotional support.

When a successful black man marries outside his race, he may get a few hateful looks from black women but his family still supports him and tries to welcome her into the family. The only major financial responsibility that women of other cultures want is a nice home and modest transportation after the wedding. This is something every successful man does instinctively; buy a nice house and cars. Most of these women are willing to have children and devote their lives to their spouse and children, trusting that this black man will take care of them for the rest of their lives. Most black women have trouble trusting black men period so they are definitely not trying to trust them with their life. The only time you see some of these black women show any concern for black love is when they see a black man with a woman of another race. They have a lot to say about that and how wrong it is for him to do that. If he was alone and spoke to them they would have treated him like he had the plague.

What should a black man who wants to fall in love and have a family do, when it appears that most black women don't trust them at all, especially when they have a lot of money? The rest of the women are so focused on trying to get money they forget about the process of falling in love or marriage. They just want the money if you want the sex. Many of these dating experiences have led to unwanted black children. These children are being used for financial gain. This perpetuates lies, cheating, and scandalous acts to get money. Good men want to avoid the drama and find someone who loves and trust him or her.

The pressure for black men to become financially responsible while dating black women before they get a chance to fall in love is running them away. The fact that the women they are running to is from another race or culture is only important to men who have made a conscious decision to only date black women. Everybody else is just looking for someone they find attractive, and everyone's view of the opposite sex is being influenced heavily by the media. It pushes; well-built thug images of black men on black women and thin, big-breasted white or multi-racial women on black men as the standard of what is beautiful. As a result, black women keep chasing the wrong type of men and black men keep marring women of other races. A lot of successful men have had a lot of contact with people of other races, whether through sports, entertainment, or business, because the top people in each of these fields are of other races. First you work together, then you eat together, then you party together, and then you sleep together. Next thing you know, you are married with children together. Love knows no race or culture and it listens to no man.

When it comes to black men who don't have a lot of money dating outside their race, we heard story after story of how unwilling black women are to support struggling black men emotionally or financially. We interviewed women to get their response and many of them agreed saying "I'm not going to help a man become successful so he can run off and marry someone else. Been there and done that." A lot of black women are tired of doing the work but not reaping the benefits once he makes it financially. I can understand their feelings, but this creates an advantage for women of other cultures who have not had that experience with black men and are more than willing to support him with every resource they have. This further proves the importance of entering each relationship without baggage. Judge a person on his or her merits. Otherwise, they will seek a fresh start with someone who won't prejudge them based on past experiences. Today, that someone is a woman of another race. If black women want black men to stop marrying outside the race, they need to focus more on being what men are looking for in a wife. Don't prejudge him based on your past experiences or the myths about black men and save all the financial demands for after the wedding.

It's not your fault

It's not your fault that black men are the way they are, but only you can make us the way you want us to be.

In this world of Players, Pimps, and Hoes,
It's not about relationships; it's about those
Who ball to they fall sipping Crystal.
Into the morning hours or until last call for alcohol
For men and women in their 20's
It's about those who want and have plenty.
Everyone has embraced this philosophy and there lies the challenge.
Women vs. Men both, trying to gain material or sexual advantage.
Everything is designer this and name brand that,
Flashier and more expensive cars,
$100 to get into bars,
And let's not forget the V.I.P because I want all the niggas and hoes to see me.
It's more emphasis on the bling bling of 5 carrot earrings,
24" rims and platinum, diamonds or gems,
Cars sitting outside the club with new shoes called dubs,
Everybody is focused on that and forgot about love.

But now it's hard to watch us invest our money in cars while our own children starve.
Walking the street draped in Ice while, little black
Children scratch out their hair trying to remove the lice.
Wishing they could read and write
Hoping and praying that their daddy might

Call, come see them or write
A letter proclaiming that in a short period of time he'll be
back and things will be fine
But instead daddy is at the club
Or driving down the street on Dubs.
Trying to find another girl to impress
But not willing to invest
In his child's potential, to be his or her best.

There was a time when black women took no shit. If you were
not a man responsible enough to commit,
Her sweet love and body you could not get.
If you did not have a job that was legit,
She would have to stay away from you and it.
Women got tired of carrying the weight of the world and
just wanted to have fun and be party girls.
Find any man who would make her burdens go away her
rent, car, and phone bill, he could pay.
Designer cloths, bags, and jewelry, he could buy luxury
cars to let her drive.

Well my grandmother did not work,
Her house, car and phone bills were perks,
Designer cloths, bags and jewelry she did get
But she didn't have to kick it, without commitment
Not with a pimp or player, nor was she a whore,
What she did was find her a husband to adore.
A man that stepped to her correct
Because she had standards that demanded respect.
For that he tried to give her the world
He gave her a ring to prove she was his only girl.
That is the life she knew until she died,
He lived just waiting to join her by her side.

Let's follow the examples of our great grandparents.
They understood the importance of love and marriage.
If it was not for their desire to push baby carriages
We wouldn't be here with our lofty goals to live lavish.
Your yesterdays influence your today and your today
influence your tomorrows
And at this pace all I see in our future is pain and sorrow.

By Chris Cokley

"Most of the women I ask the question, "Has a man ever asked you to marry him?" the answer was yes and it took place when they were in there twenties. Most said they were not ready, they wanted time on their own to get to know themselves and what they really wanted."

II. THROUGH THE EYES OF GOOD MEN

In this section, we will explore some of the internal mindsets and external forces that are working overtime in the African American community. We have the spotlight of the media on the Hip-Hop culture, highlighting the musical talent of our youth, while exploiting the growing disrespect for black women. Let's not forget the encouraged independence of the black women. That has her asking herself everyday "Why do I need a man?" while the yearning in her heart for a man grows stronger and stronger each day. We find ourselves in an economic and sexual quandary.

The 20s: A Missed Opportunity to Find Love

At twenty-one for some and twenty-five for others, college was over and it was time to get serious about life. Some women made a conscious decision to not focus on getting married until after they established themselves in the career of their choice.

They wanted to reap the fruits of their labor on their own, so that it would not be misunderstood that a man helped them get there. This mindset would dominate the twenties for most women. Most of the women I ask the question, "Has a man ever asked you to marry him?", the answer was yes and it took place when they were in their twenties. Most said they were not ready, they wanted time on their own to get to know themselves and what they really wanted. The twenties were looked at as a time to date as many men as you can and enjoy the process. So they dated the type of men that they knew they would not marry, such as the bad boys who are free spirited. Men who would not demand a lot of time from them; I think the term is maintenance men. That meant they could stay focused on a career of their own. These men have no concept of commitment or love.

It's all about fun and sex. Woman finding it difficult to move in and out of relationships with no stability in their lives would began to fall for these men. They knew these men were not good for them long range when they initially choose these guys to play with. A lot of women had children by these men, in hopes of settling these men down and keeping them in their life. But as we all know this did not work and we created a huge number of single parent homes. Most women will say it was a mistake, not a plan to get pregnant, but really how do you make a mistake and get pregnant in the 21st century with the accessibility and knowledge of birth control? Whether it was conscious or unconscious might be in question, but a mistake I think not. In order to develop a tough skin, women became the heartbreakers, letting men know up front that they were not looking for a relationship.

This mindset was created to shift the power that men once had, to women who can now play the game with as many men as they please. In theory, this made women feel better about having control or treating men the way they feel men had treated women in the past. I can't understand how it works. If all men want is sex and all you give them is sex, how did you actually hurt them or did you just give them exactly what they wanted? One of the things that use to help men mature and begin to commit in relationships, was the guilt that they would begin to feel if they had to lie and deceive women to be with them. The hardest thing a man had to do was lie to a woman and tell her he loved her. And women made every man say it before she would be intimate with him or at least soon after. If the relationship ended because of something he did, she would cry and say, "But you told me you love me. How could you lie to me?" This would deeply eat at really good men until they could no longer continue the charade. Now men don't have to worry about this anymore. Most women let men off the hook, because women don't believe men are capable of love, so they demand money.

I'm going to let you in on a secret. The only reason men work hard to get money is to get women. Men don't mind giving their money to women who they are having sex with, especially if they have money to burn. The more money the man has, the more he is willing to spend on women these days. I will elaborate on this point in more detail later. But it is the opposite for a good man in his twenties. This is a time when he is looking for a wife, a partner, and a soul mate. Men are visual and women are usually their most attractive in there twenties for a variety of reasons, such as sexuality, ambition, passion for life. All these characteristics are attractive to men. Also, if they don't already have children, they hope the women are willing to have their children and they believe she will snap back in shape and still be a visually beautiful woman to them.

Some men still continue to chase women who are in there twenties long after the men have reached their thirties and forties. Most don't stop dating young women until they just can't take the pain of the games that women in their twenties play and they can't afford the price it costs to play. Now bad men who do not want to commit have a different approach to women who seek money and don't love or trust them. Since men believe it's the money that most women are looking for, they do everything but tape it to their cloths to exploit women.

Ladies, look at what men are having you do for a dollar. Is it worth it? Men are wearing overpriced designer cloths while driving over priced cars, wearing over priced low quality diamonds on their neck, wrist and ears, while drinking over priced liqueur in the clubs. Men do all this just to impress women to get them to have sex. Now I don't have a problem with how a brother spends his money, because I definitely like nice things. It drives me crazy to see sisters of all ages and backgrounds get caught up in this mess, using money as the only prerequisite for picking a baby daddy, boyfriend, or husband. Most of these men pretend to like you when they really resent that when you look at them, all you see is money. This causes them to use women like toys and throw them away after they're done. When they are ready to settle down, most of them look for the girls who loved them when they were broke and marry them.

Now, I'm going to take some of you into a world you may not know anything about and others will be right at home seeing themselves in every line. Some of you won't believe that there are women who live like this. Hip-Hop culture has created opportunities for so many men and women, some good and some bad. We as a people have suffered so much from material deprivation that the drive to attain money and a quality of life like the rich and famous sets us on a path ending in the destruction of black love.

"Women learned quickly that while the men hustled on the street to make ends meet, they would have to hustle the men to make ends meet. This created a segment of women motivated to achieve one primary goal, to get money from men by any means necessary."

How the Hip-Hop Culture Redefined Dating

I don't want this chapter to at all appear to place blame on the Hip-Hop culture for all the problems we face in relationships. A lot of what the culture magnified was problems that already existed in a smaller percentage in our community. The terms gold digger, pimp, bitch, and hoe all existed in our communities long before Hip-Hop came along. But by glamorizing the street lifestyle, it meant glamorizing the good and the bad. The greatest bad in our community was and is the black male and female relationship.

The Hip-Hop culture has had a lot of positive and some negative effects on African American culture or lack thereof. I'm just going to focus on the things that have affected relationships in the community. The purpose of this segment is to give those of us who left our old neighborhoods and folks not from the hood some background about where this culture took root and began to grow. I want us to all understand what took place in the lives of a large majority of our generation and how it affects us today in a lot of areas but, specifically relationships. The rise in poverty and the decrease in opportunities for Generation X, which if you were born after 1965 you are a part of, ushered in the mindset of acquiring things by any means necessary. If the only way they can see themselves taking care of their families and live the American dream is to hustle in the streets, that is exactly what they are going to do. Because the drug trade is so dangerous, most women are not allowed to participate on a significant level and most don't want to. The women would rather take drugs to make the suffering of living in poverty go away than to sell them to our children, although both concepts had devastating affects on the community. Women learned quickly that while the men hustled on the street to make ends meet, they would have to hustle the men to make ends meet. This created a segment of women motivated to achieve one primary goal, to get money from men by any means necessary.

Many rappers openly admit they sold drugs or hustled some type of way to make ends meet before or during their pursuit of money and fame in the music business. This meant the women with whom they were associated were women exposed to the hustle. Most either had a drug habit or were very poor in the hood and would do whatever it took to make ends meet. When all else failed, they could sell the one thing that will always have value to men, and that is sex. Sex in the hood is openly traded for money, drugs, or sometimes just for the privilege to hang with the hustler at the club or ride in his fancy car. That's why the Hip-Hop culture seems to have a strong disrespect for women, calling them bitches and hoes. In the early years, however, these were the only types of women who would date men in the hustle game.

Eventually, women of all backgrounds and social status found themselves attracted to and dating men who have illegal careers and no one seems to care.

Even the parents began to turn their heads the other way while their sons made a lot of money in the illegal trade business. Since most homes in the, African American community are headed by single parent mothers, this would also change the way they viewed women. I remember trying to bring a toy or a bike home that my mother did not buy. She would find out where I got it and make me take it back. If she thought I did something illegal to get it she would kill me. Now we have mothers living in Section 8 apartments with luxury furniture, big screen TVs and driving luxury cars that their sons and in some cases daughters, bought them with illegal money. This helped create the perception that young men have about women. From his mother to the girls on the street, as long as he is making money that's all women care about.

Currently, we have a generation of men who feel like nobody cares about them, just the money they make. Now the so-called good girls, and in some cases the parents of these young men are willing to overlook illegal activity for gain. Not only did the hustler loose respect for women, but the good guy watching this happen began to loose respect as well. Some women of all backgrounds and social levels began to measure men by the standard of the hustler; how much money does he have, and what kind of car does he drive.

There was a time that if you went to jail, good women would not be interested in you. Now it is looked at as sexy and hardcore. Women are being told to get a thug in their lives. Black women are the fastest growing cases of HIV in the country. I would guess, part of the reason for that is the acceptance of black men who've been incarcerated. Jail is the place where many black men are exposed to a secret lifestyle of bisexuality. Some black men are raped and forced to rape other men to survive in jail. Now if you had to live in that type of environment for ten years, or ten weeks, what would you do? How do women expect them to have no skeletons when they come out? No man will admit to being raped or rapping someone else, and any habit you maintain for 21 days or more is hard to stop. I'm not saying that all men who go to jail are rapped or decide to become bisexual. The truth is that we may never know what happens to what percentage of men who come from prison systems. Life Insurance companies won't insure men who have been incarcerated because of what they call a high-risk lifestyle. Yet this lifestyle is exactly what the media is encouraging our young men to pursue and our women to crave, the image of a thug. I'm not saying that men from prison are the sole reason for AIDS statistics or bisexuality in the African American community, just one of many high-risk behaviors some women overlook when choosing a man.

As more women were treated like bitches and hoes due to an unadulterated desire for a man's money, women became motivated to look for ways to make money on their own. Unfortunately, their choices of careers didn't change how they were treated. The rise in the popularity of strip clubs, nude bars and the African American adult movie industry all willing to employ black women regardless of education and background, all promising money and fame. The drug addicted and poor young women were willing to dance nude or have sex on camera first. It soon progressed to college students working their way through higher education.

The adult entertainment business became a multi-billion dollar industry. How do you think the good men felt watching the so-called 'good women', college educated women turning to the adult entertainment industry to make money? Once again, men began to wonder how far women would go to get money.

Remember from the earlier chapters that the hustlers and drug dealers were not the popular people in school. This probably accounted for the lack of female attention they received growing up. But now they have money, drugs, or a nice car and now women want to be with them. Part of them loves the attention and part of them resents the fact that in some cases the very same people who would not talk to them in school will now do anything to be with them. So they exploited the situation almost as payback. As a result, when music videos became popular they portrayed these women as bitches and hoes. Similarly, this is how they knew them in the hood.

A lot of people complain about the images that appear in videos not realizing that this was the only exposure they had to women, because all the descent women moved out the hood to go to college or to pursue whatever dream they had. Unfortunately, when these women returned to the hood they no longer cared where the money came from anymore, just how could they get down. This made the hustler even more powerful because he could get all kinds of women.

Now let me address the specific connection and effect these industries have on relationships in the African American community. The strip club, nude bar, or Gentlemen's Club had a huge influence on young men and women in our community. Here was a segment of this generation of men who had been ignored by beautiful women all their lives. Now they could go to a club, get in for a small fee, $10 for example, and watch women get completely naked. For a $1 tip they could even make a request.

Fifteen years later, these clubs have become the most popular hag outs of young men. Women have begun to go as well. The price really has not gone up. You can still get into a strip club for $10 and tip $1 at a time. However, you can get anything you want from beautiful women, flattering conversation, to sex like a porn star. The goodies you get depend on how much money you're willing to spend.

To make extra money, a lot of women would do bachelor parties on the side. So men would go to the clubs and recruit the women they felt were attractive to commit to do a bachelor party. I went to a bachelor party in the late 80s' and three very attractive women walked in to a very expensive hotel suite and performed a nude dance routine. They then stripped the bachelor and the best man and performed sexual favors on them while the rest of the partygoers watched. Every guy who attended was asked to contribute $50 per person to cover the food and liquor, as well as the $150 per girl for entertainment.

Now fast-forward ten years to the late 90s. I attended a bachelor party at someone's home and every guy was asked to contribute $20 for food and liquor. Three very attractive women walked in and performed a nude dance routine and offered sex to anyone in the room for $50 per man. Quite a few men took advantage of the offer. These women had sex with 3 and 4 men each and one had a line of at least ten men waiting on their chance to be with her. As you can see from this example, ten years later the women are ten years younger and nastier. And because of increased competition, the price just keeps getting cheaper. This and many other examples of parties taught a generation of men to look at women as objects who would do anything for a dollar. The patrons of strip clubs range from ages 18 and up, from all backgrounds married and single, rich and poor. Women who worked in this industry came to believe that all men were nasty, cheap and unfaithful.

Since these clubs became the major recruiting ground for women who would dance half nude in music videos, young girls started to look at stripping as a legitimate career step to acting, videos, modeling, and movies. A small number of cases exist when a dancer has made an appearance in a video or become a movie star. Most women, once exposed to this lifestyle, found out it promoted drugs, sex for money, and bisexuality. Most would never view dating in the traditional sense again. Some would swear off men all together and others would decide to only use men for money.

Two, sharp brothers who are single and active on the dating scene shared a story that blew us away:

> *My name is Mike. I met a lovely lady who I had been talking to on the phone and had been out on three dates with over the course of a month. Her name was Isha. The last time we talked on the phone we planned a tentative date for a Saturday night. She asked me to invite a friend of mine because she had a friend who was visiting her for the weekend. So I invited my*

boy, Bryant, to join us for dinner to meet her friend. Bryant and I arrived at Isha's house to pick her and her friend, Tia, up for our date. We were looking good, smelling good, and bearing flowers. After all, I really liked Isha and from the description she gave of her friend, Tia, Bryant was very excited about meeting her.

Once we arrived, Isha opened the door and let us in. Then she ran in the back room to finish getting ready. Moments later, two of the sexiest women on the planet came walking out of the bedroom door. We jumped to our feet to present them with the flowers we had purchased for them and were shock by their response that they could not remember the last time a brother bought them flowers. Isha turned to Tia and said," I told you these are real men we're going out with tonight." Isha grabbed my hand and we proceeded to the Escalade. When I glanced back Tia, followed suit and grabbed Bryant's hand. We opened the doors of the SUV for them and walked around the other side and jumped in ourselves. Isha mentioned that she wanted to go to her favorite seafood restaurant. Everyone agreed and we were on our way. Tia expressed *how happy she was with her date, Bryant, and how handsome he was and how much fun she intended to have. Isha said to Tia, "Don't do anything I wouldn't do." Tia replied, "I guess anything goes." and gave Bryant a kiss. I yelled out, "You two, be good back there." Isha playfully scolded, "Leave them alone. You just need to worry about what I'm going to do to you when we get back to the house."*

Everyone appeared to be hitting it off and flirting all the way to the restaurant. At the restaurant we continued to talk and have a great time flirting for a couple of hours. We spent almost $300 on food and drinks before they suggested that they wanted to take us someplace different. We asked where we were going and Isha replied with a laugh "Someplace special we like to go from time to time." Before we knew it, we were pulling up in the parking lot of an adult novelty store. "Why are we going in here?" I asked somewhat surprised. Isha responded, "To pick something up for later tonight." They flirted with us the entire time pulling us into the booths in the back to watch adult movie clips and shopping for all types of toys for couples' *pleasure. The ladies picked a few things up and hinted that it was time for us to go back to the house. Of course, we paid for the items they decided they wanted. We jumped back in the SUV and started on our way to Isha's house, flirting and kissing all the way.*

As we pulled up to the house, opened the doors for them and walked them up the pathway to Isha's house, their attitudes began to change. They treated us at the door like we just met, giving us final pecks on the cheek and rushed into the house without even inviting us in. They said they were tired and hoped we could do it again sometime in the near future. Bryant and I were very confused and stunned that the night ended so abruptly and could not figure out for the life of us what went wrong.

It wasn't until the next day that Isha would call me and I immediately questioned her about the date and why it ended so coldly. We met for lunch and she proceeded to tell me that she has dated men and women in her past and she was not sure she wanted to have a relationship with a man. Tia was her girlfriend and they are only having sex with each other right now. They wanted the toys from the adult novelty store for themselves. She even had the nerve to ask me to be patient and give her more time.

Of course I walked away and never called her again. I was disappointed and appalled that she would play me like that after all the long conversations we had about what we wanted in a potential partner. She lied to me from the time I met her. Even her job was a lie. She was not a secretary, but a stripper in a local gentlemen's club. Her friend Tia, was a dancer as well. We found out what club they danced at and went with a few friends one night to watch them both dance nude but would not tip them at all. I did not hear from her again for over a month. She then called me and asked me would I give her money to pay her rent. Of course I said no. Isha proceeded to argue with me asking "Why don't men just want to help without expecting sex? My response was, "Why don't women want to have meaningful relationships without expecting money?"

Sadly, this generation has learned almost everything about sex from the adult movie industry. It really took off for black women as a career choice with this new market of American males craving more ethnic adult movies. The women who became adult stars were also recruited in some cases from the strip club environment. If not, then they were introduced to the gentlemen's clubs as another outlet to make money as a featured dancer or celebrity dancer. These movies promoted images of casual sex with strangers, lesbian sex, group sex, gang bangs, male/male/female, and female/female/male as well as oral and anal sex as normal sexual behavior for our youth. This became the type of sexual activity our young men came to expect from teenage women. Women in turn aimed to please, and now all these practices are considered normal. Some of these sexual behaviors are considered high risk, for AIDS and other sexually transmitted diseases, if done without proper protection. Such factors I'm sure have allowed AIDS to remain the number one killer of black women between the ages of 18 to 24 in this country.

I drove down the street and came to a light next to a SUV with TVs in every headrest playing adult movies for everyone to see. The occupants of the vehicle were not at all embarrassed. They were hanging out the windows. Our young men don't look at sex as an act of love and intimacy, but as entertainment. If you did the research you would be amazed at how many adult movie stars have appeared in rap music videos, which further encouraged young women to aspire to this profession as a stepping-stone to success. This further confirmed in the minds of men that women would do anything for money and gave them an idea as to how freaky women would get for money and fame.

Also, the adult movie industry continued to encourage women into a bisexual lifestyle or at the very least, swear off men as nothing more than a source of money and casual sex. Now, you may ask, "What does this have to do with me? I'm not a part of this culture." Well, it's simple. When good women began to take themselves out of the dating arena, to pursue their careers it left a void to be filled by women of the Hip-Hop culture. So, all men who were looking for love were left to search among these women because they could not find you. Men of all ages who date women between the ages of 21 and 35 find that eight out of ten are a product of the Hip-Hop culture I just described directly or indirectly. Men who have come through this system and have been reprogrammed on how to date have regressed. They no longer believe that they must have intellect, charisma, and chivalry nor do they have to commit to women anymore.

The women of the Hip-Hop generation don't want to commit to one guy. That would limit their resources. They don't believe a man would be faithful anyway so they just date, kick it, or just have a special friend they sleep with as long as he is spending the money. (It was an unwritten rule that you don't date professional men because they tend to be cheap. Date the hustlers and athletes because they make their money fast and easy and they spend it fast and easy. But now the professional men have given in and they pay as much as the next man) Consequently, men have come to believe all they need to have is a lot of money and they can get any women to do anything. As a result of the Hip-Hop culture's effect on our community, there are five types of men and five types of women. They are Pimps, Players, Hoes, Bitches and everybody else falls in the category of good men and women who are frustrated and have quit dating or they're looking outside of their race to find a spouse.

"Today, teenage prostitution is at an all time high. The average age is 13 years old, some being as young as 9 years old. The number one places where pimps are picking up these young girls are the shopping malls across the country."

Players, Pimps, Hoes, Bitches

As a result of the redefinition of relationships by the Hip-Hop culture, we have turned words that were inherently negative like hoes, bitches, players, and pimps into banners of honor. Women now call each other hoes and bitches as a way of recognizing their skill level in exploiting men. And men recognize each other's accomplishments for exploiting women with player or pimp as the title.

Also, there is a whole group of people who are self-proclaimed bitches, hoes, pimps, and players. We have found that people do more for recognition and praise from their peers and family than they do for money. We have a generation of men and women striving to achieve these titles that have become the titles to represent you're at the top of the food chain when it comes to the opposite sex.

The truth is that nothing has changed about these titles since their creation. Most people would be amazed at how many women believe that sex should not be free and that if they're going to have sex, they should be compensated in some way for it. (This mindset makes you a hoe or prostitute). A lot of men have come to believe that dating is a waste of time and money. Therefore, get to the point and give her the money in cash, gifts, and entertainment or pay her bills. This makes you a Player or better known as John or

Jane - someone who solicits female or male prostitutes. Both men and women are out there paying to be with someone to whom they are not married. The only thing being discovered when a man meets a woman is how much money is it going to cost him to get her to have a relationship with him. This negotiation would go unmentioned initially. The man would take the women to dinner then try to have sex with her. If that does not work, he will buy gifts and more dinners and continue the process until he achieved his objective.

And the same happens with women who desire a relationship with a man. She will pick up the check for dinner and purchase gifts for a man until he commits to a relationship with her. Many women have decided that it does not matter if he is married, has a girlfriend, or just sleeps around. As long as he takes care of her financial and physical needs, it's okay. There are men who feel the same way about the women with whom they are having sex. (This would make you a Pimp - someone who lives off the sexual efforts of other people as their source of income. Some provide the work and others just drop you off on the corner. But when they come back, you better have their money). There are both men and women who have someone whose bills they pay, or are letting this person live in their home playing playstation2 all day, while they work to pay the bills.

This has caused men to be cheaper and more direct with dating. Now, a woman has to make up her mind rather quickly or he is going to move on and invest his time and money in someone who puts out faster. Women too, no longer take their time to date and get to know someone. They want a fast commitment or they are going to invest their time and money in someone else. This has driven men and women to compete against each other. Women to see how much money they can get from men and men to see how much sex they can get from women. This game has been around for a very long time, way before Hip-Hop was thought of, but the game has changed. Women attempt to get as much from men as they can without having sex with men. Simultaneously, men attempt to have sex with as many women as they can without spending any significant amounts of money on them. The most successful women and men at playing this game were considered at the top of the food chain in dating, the lovers and players.

Now, the game is women get as much money as you can by any means necessary, including the freakiest sex. Men have sex with as many women as possible by any means necessary, including as much money as you can afford to spend. The problem with the new rules are that the prettiest and most sexually free women, and the men with the most disposable income, irrespective of how they make their money or how attractive they look win every time. Ironically enough, they have become the role models for the next generation. Attractive men and women willing to have sex with any man or woman willing to pay the price is a prostitute or a hoe. A man or woman who pays money to have sex with someone is a John or a player. The moral of this scenario is a large majority of women are acting and at the very least thinking like prostitutes. While men are doing what men has since the beginning of time and that is support prostitution to the fullest.

For example, some women are sleeping with multiple men in one day and some refuse to kiss to avoid emotional attachment. Additionally, some request money and gifts before or after each sexual encounter. Men have become nothing more than Johns to these women. They are emotionless objects that provide money and physical stimulation for as long as they can afford to play the game. Once dismissed, the women move on to the next guy with money to spend.

Today, teenage prostitution is at an all time high. The average age is 13 years old, some being as young as 9 years old. The number one places where pimps are picking up these young girls are the shopping malls across the country. Shopping malls are the most noted place where a young girl goes to window-shop for designer clothes, shoes, and jewelry that entertainers and ghetto superstars are wearing. She stands there wondering how will she ever be able to afford nice stuff like that. Then a pimp comes along and offers to buy it for her if she would be his girlfriend. She has no way of recognizing this is wrong, because most guys look like pimps and most women encourage excepting expensive gifts from strange men they meet.

She is now caught up in a lifestyle she can't afford to maintain on her own. He is taking her to nice restaurants, driving her around in his expensive cars and treating her like an adult while making her believe he is really falling in love with her. So she starts to believe all her dreams have come true and is the happiest and luckiest girl in the world. All her friends envy her for getting a rich, older guy. This is when he starts to implement his plan. First, he exposes her to the freakiest sex by showing her porno movies and convincing her to do what she sees on the tapes. Then he adds another girl to their sexual relationship. Thirdly, he adds his friends to their sexual relationship, inclusive of drugs and alcohol. If at anytime she objects, he threatens to take her new lifestyle away and send her back from where she came. Before you know it, he has turned her out and has her believing it is only fair that she go out and make some money to help maintain their lifestyle. Besides, what else can a girl 13 years old do to make money immediately other than prostitution? After all, it doesn't seem so bad because she has already gotten drunk and had sex with strangers with him before for free.

A lot of people will stand in judgment of these young women, but substantial change in someone's lifestyle can be extremely psychologically controlling and damaging if taken away abruptly.

Why do you think alimony and palimony laws were created? If you're an entertainer who earns 30 million dollars a year and marry someone who earns 30 thousand dollars a year, of course they are going to quit their jobs and begin to live a 30 million dollar lifestyle. If 9 months later the entertainer wants a divorce and the person they married has to return to their old lifestyle, this has been proven to be too damaging. So the entertainer making 30 million a year is made to pay alimony or palimony to their ex-spouse, sometimes in the millions of dollars a year, to maintain the lifestyle to which they made the ex-spouse accustomed.

But there are no laws to protect that 13-year-old with an immature mind from her feelings of fear, pain of loosing this new lifestyle, and the love of the first man to show her some adult attention. Before you know it, she has lost all control of her ability to determine right from wrong. We are at fault for setting up our young girls to be victims of prostitution. Both men and women are at fault for making material things like designer clothes and expensive cars the most important things a young girl should aspire to attain and the fastest way to get it is from a man.

Most of you will jump up and deny that you contributed to this horrible crime. But ask yourself a few questions. Do you wear expensive clothes, shoes, handbags, and drive an expensive car? It does not matter whether you bought them for yourself or not. Do you also live by the philosophy that you only date men who can do more for you than you can do for yourself? If you answered yes to these two questions, it appears that these young girls just want to look like you and find a man like you want. And men who aspire to look like, dress like, talk like, and act like the pimps who exploit these young women for sex and money calling themselves pimps. They need to think about the messages they are sending to young men and women of this generation as well as the next.

Not everyone will have a chance to make it in the entertainment industry or go to college and get a good job. As a matter of fact, less than 10% of the African American population in this country can afford to purchase expensive clothes, jewelry, accessories, and cars. Everyone else is in debt, or stealing, lying, and manipulating someone else to buy it for them. That is when they realize that pimping and prostitution are professions which really are profitable and don't require any formal education, money or an age requirement to start. Sadly enough, it is probably the fastest way they are going to get money to change their lifestyles.

So were does all this leave a whole group of people who don't want to play this game at all? The answer is frustrated. You see prostitutes and Johns had special places and ways to meet each other. They understood why each of them was there. Now that the mentality is mainstream, you have no way of knowing if you're meeting women or men who have their lives together or people who think like prostitutes and Johns until you begin dating them.

Also, you can still run into the old school lovers and players who still play the game by the old rules. They'll spend your money without giving you sex, and get as much sex from as many women as possible without love, commitment, or money. The objective for those of you who don't want to play any games, and would like to meet someone with which to spend the rest of your lives in love and passion, is to identify the game players and eliminate them from the prospective mate list. Don't spend too much time, effort, energy, or money on these people.

Does Dating Begin or End in Your 30s

The thirties have become a difficult time for unmarried men and women who want to get married and have children. If you are anything like me, you knew at a young age that you wanted to be married, successful and have children. I made it no secret and have always said that I wanted to settle down and have five children, today I would settle for two. Now at 36 years old, I find myself single again, successful and without children. I constantly ask myself these questions: "Were did all the time go?" and "What went wrong?"

Ladies, I have a couple of questions for you. Did your mother ever tell you when you were a little girl, "Don't trust little boys because all they want is one thing."? Or, say to you, "You have to stay focused, so you can be independent and you won't need a man for anything." *You can give a little head nod to show you're in agreement.* Now is she ranting, "Girl when are you going to get married and have some children? You're not getting any younger."

What's wrong? What was once looked at as a good thing, having no children if you are not married, is now treated like a disease. Everybody wants to know what's wrong with you, instead of congratulating you for doing what you were told. Contrary to popular belief, men are under the same pressure. I'm a 36-year-old man with no children and my mother tells me every time she sees me, "I'd like to see my grandchildren before I die." My family has even become gender specific. Both of my sisters have two daughters which means it is up to my brother or me to not only have children but to have sons, grandsons, nephews. It's up to us to keep the family name alive.

As I talk to men and women who are in their thirties or older who don't have children and are not married, they all seem to say the same thing. "I did not intentionally plan to delay marriage or children, it just hasn't happened yet. Or "I have not met the right person." The truth is, it has not been their main focus. We usually get what we focus on, which is why so many more women are successful, but so few are married.

In the 1950s, Black men earned three times the amount of money black women earned. Today, the difference in average income is only a few thousand dollars. But at what price? In 1950, 65% of African American adults were married as opposed to 42% today. Today's 42% of marriages are being met now with a staggering divorce rate.

Society tells us, "You don't need someone else to be happy," and that "you must make yourself happy before you can make someone else happy." So we take this information and settle into a single and motivated lifestyle, by throwing ourselves into our careers and seeking more money and prestige. Both men and women flaunt their titles and use their money to do all the things they should be waiting until they are married to do, like purchasing homes, expensive furniture, expensive artwork, luxury cars and traveling the world. As single people, what we should be doing is living modestly and saving as much as we can to become financially independent. When we meet that special someone, we should bring economic value to the table and not debt. The fact is men and women have so much debt, most of them can't afford the lifestyles they have chosen in an effort to make them happy.

When it comes to dating, we have begun to doubt and question everything we have experienced in the past and currently. Depending on whom you talk to, the majority of the blame is placed on the male. Why is this? Is it because they believe he has struggled financially or has been historically unfaithful?

Honestly, the answer is most women don't want to believe it's because of them. Most women would prefer not to analyze what is going on with them as a whole, only as an individual. When I talk to many of my female friends about dating experiences of other men, as well as my own, most women don't want to believe the stuff their sisters are doing. The fact that they don't believe what is happening is what is essentially keeping them from taking action. The kind of action I am talking about is the action that starts within.

Once you link pain or pleasure to that which you want to have, it begins to shape your destiny. Therein, lies the key to effective change and it answers the question, "why can't you find a good man?" Women are linking pain to dating men and pleasure to their independence. Pleasure is being linked to your career, house, car, and money instead of a man. Pain is being linked to dating, trusting, love, and in some cases, sex. If you understand this you can use this tool to virtually change any aspect of your life, especially the way you date.

Let's try a little exercise:

1) **Write down the name of any man for whom you still hold negative feelings.**

2) **Ask yourself "Why do the past actions of these people still bother me?"**

3) **Ask yourself "What good has come from hanging on to these bad emotions?"**

4) **Understand that you have given these people a lot of control over your life. Let them go!**

When a person who is no longer in your life can cause you to have and harbor negative feelings, you give that person power to keep hurting you over and over again. You have essentially given that person your permission to stop you from moving on to a healthy relationship.

So often it's been said that our environment, families, or other outside events are the main reasons why most single people are not married. The truth is it's our fault! We must change our priorities.

"Women are going to have to apply; the same characteristics that help them become successful in other areas of their lives to having a mate. The first thing we need to get back is the enthusiasm and desire to be in love which gives us the energy we need to date."

To Change Your Results, You Must Change Your Priorities!

Dating has become so serious that you hate the process rather than love it. Every dating experience makes you want to quit the whole process and a lot of men and women have stopped dating during different periods of their adult life. We get into the habit of just going to work, church, and home and most women won't date any person at those locations. They don't want to be inconvenienced by a relationship that does not work out. So to truly meet someone has to be an act of destiny and this rarely ever happens. If you do meet someone, they become a threat to your piece of mind and your schedule.

Most of the time, you're not willing to change your schedule to include someone else. When I speak to most women about their schedule, it's like this: work from 8am to 6pm including commuting, work out at the gym or at home from 6:30 to 8pm. Those who did not work out went to Bible study or some ministry in their church and a few did both. Then, they would eat dinner read a book, or watch TV. Lastly, they would prepare hair and clothing for the next day until 10pm and then go to bed. On the weekends, they'd clean the house, do the laundry, and be content to make it a Blockbuster weekend. Most very successful men don't work traditional hours so when they get off from work, most good women are asleep. If you did meet this very successful man, and he's not able talk to you after 10pm a few nights a week, it's difficult to get to know each other, much less have a relationship.

If good men and women are going to find their way back to each other, we are going to have to change. Women are going to have to apply the same characteristics that help them become successful in other areas of their lives to having a mate. The first thing we need to get back is the enthusiasm and desire to be in love which gives us the energy we need to date. We would stay up all night talking on the phone to that special someone. Love is a verb; it requires action. It is not just going to happen.

Pussy is a Piece of the Puzzle

There are a lot of women out there today who act like their pussy is made of platinum, and it very well may be. But why do you assume that men have no value? If men began to act like their penises are made of platinum and decided they are going to charge you for it, how would you feel? Where would we be? You don't have anything that any other woman hasn't got. God blessed man with the ability to create life and woman with the ability to nurture and bring life forth into the world. He made sex pleasurable so that we would desire each other and bear his fruit. In other words, be fruitful and multiply and inhabit the earth. He made sexual desire so strong that even with the pain of childbirth women would be willing to do it again. I hear women all the time complain that all men think about is sex. Now that's just not true, we think about sports, too. (Smile)

Men and women were both created with sexual desire, one no stronger than the other. The desire to procreate is a major part of our mental and physical make up. But what man has done for thousands of years is suppress female sexuality. Why, you ask? Because a sexually free woman is the most dangerous animal on this planet and she cannot be allowed to exist freely in this society. So they created two categories for women: good and bad. A good woman would not have sex before she was married. Once she was married, her husband would be the only man for the rest of her life.

She was not to enjoy sex but look at it as her duty to her husband and to bear children. Then there were bad women slaves, concubines, and prostitutes. These women were regarded as less than human, and in many cases, the spoils of war, women captured from conquered lands. Their sole purpose was to provide physical labor and sexual pleasure to the male owners. This concept was deeply rooted in the Greek and Roman societies from which a lot of America's customs and traditions, and even Christian religious beliefs, come from.

Now if a man intends to spread himself sexually among many women, he is not going to be capable of going home to his wife and satisfy her sexual desire as well. Therefore, he had to prevent her from having sexual desire so she would not seek to satisfy it with someone else. If she chose to satisfy her sexual desire outside his home, she would put at risk his family and his assets to be taken by another man. The penalty for this was death, and still is in some countries. A sexually free woman in regular society could be very dangerous because she could use sex to turn powerful men against each other. She would have the power to start wars and destroy governments, hence the story of Cleopatra. I know this sounds dramatic, but think. We had an intern at the White House almost get a president of the United States impeached for engaging in oral sex. This occurred when we are supposed to be far more open and accepting as a society than a thousand years ago. Just think, if a women has sex with a man and he falls in love with her

98

and she sleeps with his brother, she could cause them to kill each other.

That is how powerful sex is and the reason it's used to sell every major product in the world from music to cars. It has been inserted into every aspect of life. There exist a mindset that a woman who expresses her sexual desire outside of marriage is bad, and if she is going to be bad then she should be compensated for it. This rationale is held true by some of our women today. You see, once slaves were free in Greek and Roman times and were no longer supported by slave masters, they did not know how to survive other than to provide sex or labor for food, clothing, or money. This same process took place at the end of slavery in this country. Many slaves became sharecroppers and would continue to work on the plantation for food, clothing, or money. Many of the women who were forced to have sex were now offered food, clothing, or money for sexual favors.

Over the past hundred years more and more women have become comfortable with sex outside of marriage. However, in a society that still attempts to make women feel bad about it is causing women to adopt one of two mentalities: either stop having sex until you're married or if you're going to have sex, make sure you're being compensated for it with food, clothing, or money. The truth is we need to move beyond these man made mentalities and back to the natural purpose of our sexuality: for love, relationships and procreation.

If you follow the word of God, then God designed men to crave women, to populate, and have dominion over the earth. He created women to be the helpmates to men, not to be independent and self-sufficient. Of course, he created man in his image and woman from man. That means we all have the ability to do anything we set our minds to. He also created marriage to protect women from being taken advantage of and children from being financially neglected. Are you telling me that God was wrong? Or is the problem that we just don't have faith in God or marriage anymore.

The problem is not that we think about sex all the time. The problem is that in today's society, the pussy has been placed on a pedestal. It's separate from everything else in the relationship. You have friendship, honesty, respect, trust, communication and love, and then way up there above everything else we have the female body.

First of all, why do women feel like they're giving something up and all men do is take it? Sex was designed to have men and women give a piece of themselves to create life and then begin to die as our children grow. When a man ejaculates he releases from his body about 226 million spermatozoa, said to be a viscid albuminous fluid, alkaline in reaction, rich in calcium and phosphorus, also in lecithin, cholesterol, albumen, nucleoproteins, iron, vitamin E, etc.

An ounce of semen is considered to be equal in value to a man's body as sixty ounces of blood, which is where it gets most of its substance. That means other parts of the body do not get the amount of constituents it needs, specifically the brain and nervous system to function at its most efficient state. Because most of us in this country have such a poor diet and could never eat enough food in a day to replace what is lost in one ejaculation, it literally kills us every time we ejaculate. Only when a woman has a baby, does she lose the essence of life from her body. You see when a woman orgasms, it is internal. She re-absorbs her fluids into her body and she absorbs the man's fluids into her body making her even healthier if she doesn't conceive a child and the male sperm does not carry disease. This is possibly one of the many reasons that women live longer than men on average.

Sex or making love is an exchange of pleasure. Short of childbirth, men are giving of themselves more than women. Most men are very intimate people and they show their love physically. Very few men are articulate enough to truly communicate their feelings verbally. That is just not something we are taught to do and women no longer require men to articulate. Women communicate their love verbally because they have been taught that the physical is bad. That's the way it is and that's the way it's always been in this country.

A lot of women feel, that if they give their body up too soon or even at all, the man will lose interest in them. This is why they resort to playing games. Nothing could be further from the truth when it comes to the good man. When you decide to have sex with a good man with whom you have chemistry, it does not matter if it is on the first date or the day after the wedding. What matters are the sincere feelings both of you share that resulted in your decision to have sex. A good man only loses respect for a woman who uses her body for gain, whether it is pleasure or money that she seeks instead of an expression of feelings and desire.

If you want to have a strong relationship with that good man, you can't hold back anything, or it's doomed before it starts. A relationship is like making a cake. You have flour, sugar, eggs, etc. If you leave something out, what's going to happen to your cake? Or to be more precise, it's like a jigsaw puzzle where no one piece is anymore important than the other. If there's a piece missing from the top, bottom, middle, or the sides, you can't complete it. Let me ask you a question. What do you do if you can't complete a jigsaw puzzle because one piece is missing? You throw it away, although there are some people who will put all the other pieces together and let it sit there with a piece missing hoping to find it. Some of you are in bad or broken relationships. Instead of getting out, you stay and hope to find the missing piece. You never find it because the missing piece is you.

In a good relationship, you have various key components that make it work: respect, honesty, trust, communication, love, commitment, and sex. Once again, no one component is more important than the other and without them all the relationship cannot work. A man will walk away from a relationship if he is disrespected, just as fast if not faster as if you were not making love to him. Remember, sex or the giving of your body is just one piece of the relationship puzzle, not the prize.

So don't use sex to acquire material gain, because when you use sex that way, it becomes an object of barter. It's no longer an act of desire and therefore love can't grow. If he really likes you and wants to have a meaningful relationship with you, it will all come to a halt because he will no longer feel like you really care about him. His guard will go up to protect his heart and you will become nothing but a sexual object to him. Your feelings for him may start to grow, the more time you spend together and come to realize he is a good man, but he will probably remain closed to a commitment. Love is never owed, it's given freely and so is everything else associated with it. The only thing worse than having a price tag on your body, is selling your soul.

"How can your mind, body, and spirit work together too create a loving and fulfilling relationship if you have separated them from each other? You date a man for mental stimulation or financial gain, while using a toy to satisfy your sexual needs and you're lost spiritually because you know this is not how God intended it to be."

What Will It Be .... Boys or Toys

We know you can't create something out of nothing. You can't create intimacy without passion and chemistry. These things are triggered by your attraction for someone and your physical desire to be with them. Since we shouldn't just jump in the bed together, the dating process begins. "You can't turn on the engine if there is nothing under the hood." By the way, have you ever noticed how after a woman has had a bad dating experience, the first thing she changes is her view on sex? Whatever she did with the last man she is not going to do with the next one. If she slept with the last man fast, she is going to make the next man wait. If she made the last man who messed up wait, she is going to give it to the next guy quick. Or the growing choice today, which lasts on average about six months in most cases, is to stop having sex altogether.

Perhaps it's us, but we have been noticing a growing number of women proclaiming the statement, "I don't need a man, I can take care of myself." Now when they say that they're referring to something specific. Women are talking about taking care of their own sexual needs or denying them. There are various reasons why women claim they are doing this and we will elaborate on that later. But for now, let's talk about how and why this affects you finding, and more importantly, keeping a good man. Most of us are taught that independence is inherently valuable, but independence is not always positively regarded. In fact, it can appear to be down right selfish. A lot of women feel like there are advantages to pleasing themselves. For example, by not becoming emotionally attached to a man keeps the number of sexual partners low, and woman are confident that they can get the job done faster and better than most men. However, when it's all said and done, what did you accomplish? You said you wanted a good man didn't you? But, like a peacock flaunts his colors, you flaunt your ability to satisfy your sexual needs without us, never realizing you're extinguishing our most basic human need, to be wanted and desired by somebody else.

Women please put the toys down and put that time, effort, energy, and emotion into finding the right man. Taking care of your sexual needs with toys is ultimately a way of rejecting one of the things that brings us together, desire. Making love is something we were not meant to do alone. It doesn't matter how much you care for someone if you do not bother to show it because you have extinguished your natural aphrodisiac, sexual desire. Why then, should they believe you care?

Warning, the five words you're about to hear have caused more damage to male/female relationships than any other words in the English language. Whether a friend speaks them, a lover, or a person you don't even care about. They are without question the five most alarming words to men across the world, "**I DON'T NEED A MAN.**"

The human being is the most advanced instrument on the planet, with every piece working in harmony to achieve whatever it is that you ask it to do. How can your mind, body, and spirit work together to create a loving and fulfilling relationship if you have separated them from each other? You date a man for mental stimulation or financial gain, while using a toy to satisfy your sexual needs and you're lost spiritually because you know this is not how God intended it to be. Masturbation can be dangerous to your ability to have a healthy sexual relationship, which can be the reason for the entire relationship to fail.

Again, your body is one of the most advance instruments in the world and you can train it to do almost anything you want. Now if you continue over a long period of time to use outside stimulation to achieve orgasm, your body will adapt to that stimulation and only respond to that. I have heard stories from women who masturbate directly after sex with their partner because they cannot orgasm any other way anymore. Your man may go along with this because most men are just happy to be included, but you and he both know that will not do for the rest of your life together. So he never imagines himself marrying you because he does not believe he can satisfy you. The truth is, he can't and probably no man can sexually please you because no man can vibrate a thousand times a minute for as long as you want.

Rejection, whether in or out of a relationship is never easy for anyone to handle. Most times it often leads to thoughts of worthlessness, and this is how you might be making your partner feel when all you really wanted to do was get back that feeling you gave yourself last night. Sexual rejection leaves a man mentally scared of intimacy and causes serious issues to his self-confidence. I am not one to personally make a case for or against masturbation. Some studies show that masturbation may offer medical benefits to women, if you have chosen celibacy as a way of life. The desire or urge to climax is strong in both men and women and can be a great relief from stress. It is my hope that you would use your understanding of your body to enhance passion and intimacy with your partner, not for pleasuring yourself. Love is not selfish.

The Sexual Revolution: Pleasure, Power, or Love

Good men are on the outside looking in as women are waging war on love and relationships, under the title of sexual liberation. Women have decided that they no longer need a commitment from a man to enjoy sex. They have also decided they no longer need to be emotionally involved with a man to enjoy sex. Furthermore, some have even decided that they don't really need to know anything about the man to enjoy sex. Many also would rather trade in the vulnerability of love for the power in casual sex, without regard for their partner's feelings.

You see, women have decided now is the time to do to men what men have done to them for years. Now women lie to men about their feelings, use men for sex and cut off communication shortly after. Additionally, they have multiple sex partners, which sometimes includes two friends and even two family members. I heard a very popular female rapper recite a poem on TV called, "We follow your lead." She went into detail all the bad things men have done and after each one she repeated, "We follow your lead."

What good men can't understand is why would women as intelligent as they profess to be choose to follow the lead of the worst men we have instead of following the lead of men who were doing what they needed to do for their family and community. It's always easier to do the wrong thing than to do the right thing, which is the reason why so many women have chosen this mentality. The only problem with this philosophy is that it does not work.

The men you're seeking to get revenge on are actually taking advantage of the situation to use, abuse, and exploit women even more. Men who have done wrong by women for years don't have feelings for you to hurt. They don't want to be in committed relationships and they're happy they don't have to lie to you anymore. So many women are willing to have casual relationships that include sex but don't require commitment. I think you call it just kicking it with someone or having a special friendship.

Some women feel that as long as they control when, where, and with whom this casual sex takes place, somehow they have the power. This simply isn't true because men will just make sure they have enough women they are kicking it with that someone is always available when they want them to be. Some women also believe to request gifts or money in these casual relationships will give them the upper hand. Please remember that prostitution is one of the oldest professions in the world. Men have always been willing to pay for sex; you have accomplished nothing new.

So while some women are running around playing with their sexual freedom and trying to act like men, they have accomplished two things. One, they have managed to isolate and hurt the good men who are looking for a wife and partner they can respect and with whom to spend the rest of their lives. Two, they have managed to separate their sexuality from their emotions, which is extremely dangerous and in most cases irreversible.

The level of distrust and hate for men required, for a woman to give herself to someone she doesn't care about runs so deep. Women who have decided to live this way usually have no trust or faith in men anymore. Most of them will never be able to have a normal, loving relationship that includes trust, respect, honesty, and communication with a man again. This is why so many women are turning to each other for committed, loving relationships although many don't consider themselves lesbian. Whether you're a man or a woman, you should never disconnect your emotions from your sexuality because this component is essential to bonding which is essential to marriage.

"Until the wedding day comes, every man who wants to be married should be preparing himself to be a husband and father. Every woman who wants to be married should be preparing to be a wife and mother. All the decisions you make until that time should work towards achieving that goal."

What Does God Say about Dating

Nothing! The word of God provides guidance in every area of life except dating. However, it does discuss love, marriage, children, and every other aspect of life. Too many people believe that having faith means God will send you a soul mate, so they throw themselves into the church waiting for God to bless them with the man or woman of their dreams. I may be wrong, but my research says God only put together one man and one woman, and that was Adam and Eve.

He created both of them and I have yet to find any other couple in the bible that God placed together directly. Nor has He advised anyone to get married who had not planned to on his own. God has always allowed man to choose his own wife. Some have even chosen more than one wife and still God did not interfere. The word of God provides many teachings on how to build a marriage and family that honors God. One of the greatest gifts God ever gave us was to create us in His own image. He gave us the ability to love, learn, to distinguish right from wrong, the ability to choose, and the ability to reproduce.

I believe when Judgment Day comes, God will look at the choices we've made and be pleased or disappointed with how we used what He gave us. So I'm going to dare to be different and say, "Stop waiting for God to do something that He equipped you to do yourself." Use all the tools He has given you and do it right.

Women, prepare to be a wife and make yourself available so that a good man can find you and choose you to spend the rest of his life with. Men in turn, prepare to take care of a family and stop spending all your money dating and trying to impress the wrong women. When you meet the right woman, step up and make the commitment and maybe she will except and honor you by being your wife.

Until the wedding day comes, every man who wants to be married should be preparing himself to be a husband and father. Every woman who wants to be married should be preparing to be a wife and mother. All the decisions you make up until that time should work towards achieving that goal. If you're not sure what it is to be a husband and father or wife and mother, don't worry. It is in the word of God and very clearly explained. Once you know were you're going, it becomes easier to figure out how to get there.

LOVE IS

Why don't you believe in love, is it because love did something bad to you, or did you do something bad and blame it on love?

I keep hearing people say they never want to fall in love again
They equate it to committing the greatest sin.
They talk about how bad they felt the last time they were in--- love.
You see love seems to take the blame for all the relationships that don't last,
All the romances that pass
The heartache, tears, and anger that crashes
Into your life when the relationship broke like glass.

Love is the feeling that someone completes your life
That the air you share would be too much to bear
If you had to breathe it alone.
Love is a 24-hour burn in your gut that makes you think so much about the role he or she would play in your life.
Love is a mental, physical, and chemical change in your existence
That elevates you to the level of perseverance allowing you to achieve things otherwise unreachable.
Love is the willingness to take all the risk of love lost,
Believing that nothings worse than never loving at all.
Love is unconditional, unpredictable, uncontrollable and unreal.
Love is the foundation on which to build castles of dreams and fantasies that heal.

I believe most of you fear love, even hate love,
When you've never met or even dated love.
It's lust you're confused about and truly afraid of
Lust pretends to be love then it all turns old
When you don't know the person that you claim to love soul.
Lust is passion combined with physical attraction bringing about a chemical reaction that delivers temporary satisfaction.
Digging deep into your being as it attempts to fill a void
That love left or a home that loves never occupied or destroyed.

You see love is life and life is love one can't flourish with out the other.
It's as rhythmic as our heartbeat and as pure as a newborn's reaction to its mother.
To live without love is to truly die inside
Love without life is to aspire to be with the most high,
For only the most high is love without life and love eternal.
Life with out love equates to hell's inferno.
So don't live your life in vain,
Because life without love is truly insane.

By Chris Cokley

III. WHAT MEN WANT AND WOMEN NEED

Because of their nature as the provider and protector, most men have always picked their woman strictly based on how she makes him feel. Her career, income level, or level of education have not been traditional factors in his decision making process. Women, on the other hand, have traditionally had a balance between what they need in a man and what they want in a man. The reason for this balance was largely due to the financial dependence women had on the men they married. Women were not given the same opportunities as men to make a living. Today so many more women are taking care of themselves financially and are comfortable living on their own. Now women feel that they no longer need a man. They just want one. Women are no longer selecting men based on need. As a result, they pick the wrong man most of the time.

Attitudes That Cause Us to Fail at Love

The first problem we have is the way we approach relationships. Men look for women who are unrealistically beautiful with the perfect body, like the images that we constantly see in the media rather than defining beauty individually. While women look for the ideal man package, that also includes unrealistic standards of physical appearance, confidence, intelligence, financial success, etc. Silly enough, they want to be able to know if he has the package just by looking at him. The chance of a male model with the complete package and a gorgeous female model meeting is slim to none.

The challenge is most men are looking for women who look like models but they don't look like models themselves. If he finds her, she is probably not going to be attracted to him. And women are looking for male models that have the ideal package, but they don't look like a model nor have the ideal package. So if they find him, he will probably not be attracted to them. Look for what you feel you are as a person. If everybody does this and be honest with themselves, we would find the perfect partners in life.

The first attitudes we need to overcome are **ignorance and incompetence.** We must understand how to learn before we can learn. In this book, my goal is to take you through the stages of learning and how to date to find love.

The **first stage** is when you don't know that you don't know. This is the stage most people are in. They don't have a clue what it takes to be in a successful relationship although they pretend like they do.

The **second stage** is when you realize you don't know and it brings about a burning desire to find out what you don't know. This probably is the stage you're in right now which may be the reason why you picked up this book and took the time to read it.

The **third stage** is when you are practicing what you have learned although you may not have it mastered and may need to reference the book or lesson of your choice. I hope you find some of the things in this book interesting enough to try and start to have success in dating.

The **fourth stage** is when you know what you want and what type of person it will take to get you there so well that you don't have to think at all. This is the level we all hope to achieve; the moment you can tell early when meeting someone whether or not they could be 'the one'. The only danger with this level of understanding yourself and others is most of your relationships won't go pass the third date until you meet the right person. This is good because you won't spend a lot of time on people who don't have potential. Sometimes it's bad because you're lonely, although you're not alone. This sometimes can be the worst kind of loneliness. You have people in your life but no one is fulfilling your needs. But when you do meet that right person, it is the best kind of love.

The second attitude that we need to overcome is the **pain of change**. The one thing constant in life is change and you need to be prepared for it. Your life will change when the right person shows up. It will change again when you fall in love, and it will change again when you get married, and it will change again when you have children. It will change differently with each child you

119

have, and will change again when they grow up and leave home. I think you get the picture, so don't be afraid of changing your schedule to talk to someone late on the phone or to spend more time together. We tend to settle into our habits and we believe that if we meet someone, they should fit into our lives. Usually, that's not the case. Most women pass up Mr. Right because they are not willing to go through the pain of change.

The third attitude we must overcome is **lack of faith.** Women have lost faith in men and men have lost faith in women. We all seem to have lost faith in the power of love. And as much as I hate to say it, this means we have actually lost faith in God because God made man in his image and women to be his helpmate. With timeless examples of love in the Word, we should all know how important it is to love. So why don't we believe that we can find someone to love and share the rest of our lives? Faith without works is dead, so I guess I can assume there is no faith since nobody seems to want to do the work it takes to find and maintain a great relationship.

The fourth attitude we must overcome is **lack of trust.** Trust is truly the foundation of any great relationship because it is probably the most tested of the ingredients required to make it work. We live in a society that doesn't respect relationships and the image of infidelity is everywhere you look. Plus, the advancement of technology has made it easier for us to deceive each other with things like cell phones, two-way pagers, email, computers, and the like. All our friends are telling us that all men are dogs and all women are scandalous freaks. Magazines plaster stories on the covers like, "Why Good Men Cheat." This does not make sense to me because if they cheat, why do you call them good men? But anyway, it makes you feel like no one can be trusted. God forbid you take a chance on someone and they deceive you, then everyone makes you feel like you're so stupid for trusting someone in the first place.

I'm going to let you in on a technique I use to allow me to trust everyone. First, I let them know that cheating is unforgivable. So if you get caught, don't ask me if we can work it out. Then, I have an imaginary trophy for cheaters and liars called Best Actress in a Drama Series. Because drama is what they will cause you if you take them back, and they are so dramatic when they are trying to lie their way out of trouble. Everyone is allowed to win at least once, but nobody gets to win twice. The first indiscretion is totally their fault. If there is a second indiscretion, that is totally my fault. This way I don't waste any energy trying to prevent being misled the first time. I allow you to win your trophy if you so choose. Also, I have faith that anyone who treats people who care about them like that is going to get it back tenfold by someone else. Last but not least, I focus on myself so the next time they see me, I look better, feel better, and I'm doing better than when I was with them.

The last attitude we need to overcome is **lack of passion.** Passion is defined as a powerful emotion or appetite, most often applied to sexual desire. When I talk to anyone who is successful at something difficult, the word passion comes up. They all talk about how you have to love what you're doing and never give up. They all talk about the work ethic required to achieve their goals, and how it was their passion that gave them the strength to work so hard and long.

The reason most people don't have passion for relationships or more specifically, the opposite sex, is because of the last four points I just covered: ignorance, pain of change, lack of faith, and lack of trust. Such factors lead us to experience the deception of relationships without passion. Passion has been my greatest blessing. To know passion has allowed me to have an incredible life. Since I only do things passionately or not at all has allowed me to succeed in so many areas of life. And because I am a very passionate person, it allows me to identify other passionate people as well as recognize people who have no passion for life, goals, or me as a lover and friend. This blessing has allowed me to waste very little time, energy, or money on people whose intentions for me were not genuine.

The ability to be passionate, and to make it a prerequisite for anyone, who wants to be in a relationship with you, will save you from so much heartache and pain. The reason why this is so important is because people will go to great lengths to deceive you, like tell you they love you, share their bodies with you while performing the most intimate sexual acts, give you money, and spend time with your family and even your children. Some people will even go as far as marrying someone with whom they are not in love. And the truth is, they don't care about you at all. They just needed something from you and they needed you to drop your guard to get it. Most of the time they are after money, shelter, credit, and in some cases just sex. I have found one common denominator with people who enter relationships for the wrong reason. They have a difficult time faking passion because most of them don't know what it is and how it manifests itself physically. You must commit to being a passionate person in your relationships and you will weed out the pretenders and find the real deal a lot faster.

"We don't know if it's because no one has ever explained to women what good men are or if women just don't believe good men exist. We believe women have invested so much time in dating the wrong men that they have lost touch with what a good man should be like."

What Is A Good Man?

Most good men don't believe women could recognize a good man if he was standing in her bedroom. We don't know if it's because no one has ever explained to women what good men are or if women just don't believe good men exist. We believe women have invested so much time in dating the wrong men that they have lost touch with what a good man should be like. So I am going to shed some light on the subject. What I need women to do is stop thinking about what they can do for themselves while trying to find a man who can do the rest and just think of what characteristics a good man should have regardless of their situation.

Now, the tricky part of finding a good man is to know when to make an exception if a man does not have all the characteristics we are about to discuss. The answer is never to make an exception when first meeting someone. He either is or is not a good man at that moment. All men have the ability to be good men, and most men pass in and out of the good man stage many times when they are single and married, surprisingly.

The key is to only except men who are good men when you meet them and refuse to date them when they are not. This will force men who have the qualities to be good men but don't want to commit to make a decision to always be good and stay out the game. Good men don't want to be in the game, but they will, because they feel they can't trust women to be honest. The right women can turn a potentially good man into a good man by what she doesn't do rather than what she does. Don't date him until he gets his act together, which usually means when he decides to commit to one woman.

I don't think we spend enough time thinking about what is important to the opposite sex. I wish I really knew what mattered to the women of today, but I'm not quite sure. I believe I have the right idea of what a husband is suppose to be, but it doesn't appear to be what women are looking for. I think they are looking for a boy toy, a man with a body like LL, the mentality of a thug, someone who is good in bed, and has a lot of cash.

Now I'm not saying that women shouldn't have those characteristics in their men if that is what they want, but there is so much more to being a good man.

Here are the six characteristics all men who plan to be a husband and father should have before you date them.

1. A good man should be able to provide a home for you and any subsequent children. I don't mean potential to provide unless you're both still in college. He should be financially responsible now and have a plan for the future.

2. A good man should have a goal and a vision of what he wants his family life to be. If he does not want to be in a committed relationship, then he is not a good man right now.

3. A good man should be intellectual enough where you feel comfortable allowing him to make all the important decisions for the family. This may include how his money and yours should be spent, what church you will attend, and what school is best for the kids, etc. A good man would never want to make any of these decisions without his wife. The point is, you would feel comfortable allowing him if the need arose.

4. A good man should be a gentleman at all times in public and whatever you want him to be at home. Just because you want a thug in the bedroom does not mean you have to date a thug in the streets.

5. A good man should have some sense of community and be willing to provide leadership. Community is a very big part of your children's upbringing and your wife's safety.

6. A good man should be confident, secure, trusting, and focused on achieving his goals.

The six points covered should be the universal characteristics of all good men. If someone is a good man for you personally, it will require you to do a little more research to see if you're compatible. Don't compromise on these characteristics at all. They are the foundation and core of all good men.

The Traditional Role of Men and Women

It's true this information may seem to favor the man and put a lot of the responsibility to change as it relates to dating on the women. It goes back to the inherent role of the man and the women in society. If the man is to ask the woman to marry him, then it is the woman's responsibility to be someone he would want to marry. Now I guess you're probably questioning, "What about what she wants?" Well, she should only date or say yes to marry someone who is exactly what she wants. Good women should be proposed to by every man she dates, but should except the proposal of the one she loves.

Men are wired to be the providers and the leaders in a relationship. So women began to look for responsibility and leadership as two major characteristics in a man. Add to that compatibility and physical attraction and you have a potential match. Now let me elaborate on each point so that you understand how easy it is to determine if you should date a man or not. First, look at his living situation. Don't base it upon the myth that if he does not own a home, then he is not a good man. This is a fallacy.

HOW TO PICK THE RIGHT MAN

1)   Decide if he can provide for you a lifestyle you can be happy with whether or not he achieves the big goals and dreams he may have for himself. He should live alone unless he is responsible for taking care of his parents or his children. Either way he should be the one responsible for the bills. Then ask yourself if in the worst-case scenario, "Can we live in his home, apartment or find a place within the same price range he pays now and be happy?" If the answer is no, then don't date him. How many cars does he have? In the worst-case scenario, can you live with only one car? Or could he afford to get two dependable cars with the money he spends for that one luxury car? Can you live with this situation? If the answer is no, then don't date him.

2)   Look at how well he takes care of himself. Does he have quality clothes, food, and amenities? Most men will treat their women the same or a little better than they

treat themselves. If you can't live with the answer, then don't date him.

3) Make sure you're compatible by a score of 90 % or more. Look at values, spirituality, and interests in order of importance. How does he rate and what is his vision or plan for you in these areas? Take a piece of paper and number it one through seven and put in order of importance these seven values, spirituality, career, marriage, children, health, family & friends, Education & Recreation. Now have him do the same and compare. Compatibility does not mean that your list should look the same; they should complement each other. For example, career should be higher on his list than yours if you expect him to be the provider and marriage should be higher on yours to maintain a happy home. If spirituality is not number one on his list, I suggest you run. Also, compare things like hobbies, music, food, types of movies, and books. Do you like to talk, are you a morning person, like to entertain others, and any other things that are important to

you. Below is an example of what it should look like when you're done. Exchange them in each other's presence and discuss each point to be clear.

EXAMPLE:

Priorities for living a happy life

1. Spirituality – my belief in a higher power and the purpose of my life

2. Career – unfortunately we live in a capitalist society and in order for me to be a man I must be able to make a living capable of supporting a family

3. Marriage – I believe that man was not meant to be alone and that he should have a helpmate and partner in all aspects of life

4. Children – I believe that procreation is not only a choice but also a necessity for those of us who are conscious and can produce the leaders of tomorrow. Perhaps our children may find the answers that might make life easier until change is imminent

5. Health – In honor of my spirituality and family I must do everything possible to maintain a healthy lifestyle (diet, exercise, weight loss, relaxation, meditation etc.)

6. Family & Friends – I believe the future of this country and the economy will warrant family units to become a stronger base for our communities in order to survive and raise children. Friendship is essential to the soul, the few friends I have I hope will always be a part of my life.

7. Education & Recreation – During personal time I shall commit to a broad education of the history of the Liberal Arts, Sciences, Civilization, Secret Sciences, and Social Order. To do this I will be required to travel extensively. This step is actually part of the 1st step but it will take my entire lifetime to master, so it will be done in conjunction with the other steps.

A woman that would be compatible with me would have her list in this order:

(1. 1) (2. 3) (3. 4) (4. 5) (5. 6) (6. 2) (7. 7)

Compatibility

1. **Hobbies I love** – Cooking, dancing, traveling, golf, tennis, watching basketball and football

2. **Music I love -** R&B, Hip Hop, Jazz, spiritual

3. **My favorite food** – Italian, Japanese, Creole, and experimenting with multicultural dishes.

4. **Type of Books I like** – Self-help, Autobiographical

5. **Type of Movies I like** – Comedy, romantic comedy, action, karate

6. **Type of Women I love** – Sensuous, confident, compatible, beautiful inside and out

7. **My Characteristics** – Very positive, charismatic, afternoon/evening person, love to talk, high sex drive, love people and entertaining

This exercise does require you to know what you want and like to do. It would be a good idea to do this exercise before you meet someone so that you're clear about

your priorities. **Compatibility is one of the most important keys to a long and satisfying relationship. If the person you're dating will not participate, you have to wonder how interested they must be in getting to know you.**

4) **Make sure he is physically attractive enough to you, where there is nothing sexually that you would not want to do with him. He must motivate you to be willing to do the little extra work to keep the passion level high. Also, be very observant as to his attraction level for you. If he doesn't light up when you walk into a room, then don't date him. Women must stop falling for men who will sleep with you but don't find you attractive enough to marry.**

Now you don't have to date a man for a long time to find out if you are compatible in these four areas. One date, one visit to his house, a few hours of good conversation, and asking a lot of questions will let you know. If you follow these four suggestions, you can disqualify most men in two weeks and qualify most in thirty days. The reason it takes longer to qualify a man is because once he says all the right things, spend as much time with him as you can to see if his actions match his words.

What Men Really Want in A Women

Based upon my explanation of what men need to fall in love, it will take longer for him to determine if you have what it takes. I have participated in enough round table discussions with other men to have a decent idea of what a man really wants. Check out this list of what men say they want in a woman.

It does not matter if you agree or not, this is what we want!

1) **A woman who is physically attractive to him; someone who can make him feel excited every time he sees her. She must be able to look sexy without looking like a slut. Every woman can be sexy to a man if she is first sexy in her own mind. So make sure you're at your best at all times. Now sexy is not just what you wear, but how you wear it and the attitude you wear with it. A woman can be sexy in any environment from the boardroom to the bedroom with style and class. Whether you're going to the club or cleaning the house, you can be sexy. Your goal is to make him want to make love to you every time he sees you. Even if it is not your intention to make love**

to him at that time, make him think about it until it happens. You will know if you're that women for him by the way he reacts to you. He should want to touch you every time you walk by him. Now the trick to this is remembering that beauty is in the eye of the beholder. Everybody has somebody who thinks they're beautiful.

2) A woman who makes him feel like, he is the love of her life. It's security that he wants to feel. Beyond a shadow of a doubt he must feel that you don't want to be with anyone but him. Don't talk to him about your fantasy man from the movies or TV, or how perfect your ex-boyfriend was. Definitely don't tell him how you gave everything to your last love and how he broke your heart and how you don't intend to ever do that much for a man again. No man wants to marry a woman who gave her best to somebody other than him.

3) A woman who makes him feel needed on every level: mentally, physically, emotionally, and financially. He needs to

know he is capable of being able to make her dreams come true. Now don't get me wrong. He respects and appreciates a women who can do it all herself, but he wants one who does not choose too. God created women because he gave man the world and yet still he was not happy. Instead, he was lonely and needed help. Who am I to say that I don't need a woman to complete me? God created Adam in his own image, yet determined he needed Eve. During their union, Eve never questioned her need for Adam. I think we all agree they were much closer to perfection than you or I. Why is it that Christian women today claim to not *need* a man? And yes the word is need; want is nothing more than a wish. Success requires a burning desire fueled by a need. That's what will motivate you to do what it takes to survive the journey to a successful marriage.

4) A woman who is fun to be around, which means compatibility, is important. Someone who will allow the boy that still exists in the man to come out and play with

the girl that exists in the women. A true man should be seriously making decisions that matter to someone's livelihood most of his day. At some point during the day, he just wants to be a kid and he needs to feel like he can be that kid with you. If not, he will hang with the fellows more than he does with you.

5) A woman who understands the importance of food in building a family and a relationship. Know how to cook or at least be willing to learn. Every tradition in a man's life has involved food. His mother made sure of that. Making food something special with which to build family traditions in the future is a labor of love. Sure he can take you out to dinner while you're dating because that is just one meal out of the day. Knowing that his woman can cook allows him security in knowing that he and his family will be fed healthy meals everyday day. Most men do not want to have to decide what and where you're going to eat every time you're

together. We just want to eat something
good and move on.

6) A women who is fabulous sexually. She is
comfortable with her body and is unselfish
and creative with lovemaking. A reason
why some men are not satisfied sexually
has more to do with frequency than the
skill level of lovemaking. When a man
thinks about sex, he should be thinking
about what you did earlier or anticipating
what you're going to be doing with him
later that night. Possibly, some of you are
reading this and saying nobody wants to
have sex that much. Remember, I'm not
just talking about intercourse. I'm talking
about intimacy.

7) A woman who is financially responsible. It
doesn't matter how much money a women
makes as long as she is living within her
budget. This shows him that you are
responsible with money and will do what it
takes to make sure that ends meet. He
must also know that you are going to be
responsible with his money once you're

married and you become his partner. This also shows him that his financial contributions will be appreciated, not expected. Once you are married, then you should expect to be taken care of financially, but not before.

8) A woman who is family adaptive, one who can blend into his family and have a relationship with his parents and siblings. If you are comfortable around them and display genuine love and concern for his family, they too, will love you and will be accepting of you. For this to happen his family needs to see that you love each other, they will embrace you with open arms. Warning: don't meet the parents unless you are in love. Too many people are trying to include their families in the process of selecting a potential mate. The worst thing you can do is include someone in your relationship on any level, including your children, until you feel absolutely sure you're both in love. Some men are guilty of taking women home to the family too soon. Don't let him do that to you. You only get

one chance to make a first impression. Let yours be love. If you're not sure that you're in love with each other, don't meet the parents.

Now as simple as the eight things are, it's very difficult to find women who will meet all eight requirements at the same time. All women have the ability to display these eight characteristics for the man she chooses. But most self-proclaimed, good women only display four out of eight criteria men are seeking. That is sometimes enough to get a man into the relationship, but it's not enough to get him to commit and marry you.

I'm going to let you in on a secret. The most important of the eight when you first start dating to get him to fall in love is what I call the 4 F's. They are: fun to be with, financially responsible, fantastic food, and fabulous sex. Some of you are uncomfortable with the last point, fabulous sex. It is last because this 'F' is optional and contingent upon similar lifestyles if sexual activity or celibacy.

I don't think sexually active men should date sexually inactive women and vice versa. But if you agree to be sexually active, be fabulous at it or don't do it at all. You can be safe and fabulous at the same time, too. Now most women still don't get more than two points out of the four criteria at the same time. This is the

143

reason why some men cheat and women can't understand it. Have you seen or heard of a situation when a man cheated. The women he was with didn't look as good as his woman, nor did she have as much going for her? As a woman, you may wonder why. What does she have that I don't have? I'll tell you, she's the girl not worried about the stress of a career, bills or a whether her man is faithful.

She learned how to cook out of necessity because she either had some younger siblings to care for or already has children to feed. She's the girl who loves sex and will do the freaky stuff anytime and anyplace. She is happy and appreciative if you take her out or just come to visit her and do something simple like paying for her hair and nails to be done every once in a while. She just wants to have fun, not fight. This is why men are cheating. It's the first four points. She may never display the other four items to get him to marry her, but she can make him happy if only for one night. And she does it by accident, by being herself with no idea of what a man wants. It's more of what the situation dictates that gives the edge to the other woman.

Now that you know, don't let another woman get the edge in your relationship. You most be the girlfriend, the wife, and the mistress. It will take approximately three to six months of dating to see if you have the first four characteristics, and six months to a year to determine if you have all eight areas covered.

If you have all the eight areas covered at the same time and he has your ten areas covered, then be patient and enjoy. If it has been more than twelve to eighteen months and he has not proposed by then, move on. He has a problem with commitment. But be sure all areas are covered! The reason why it is so important that you be thorough with these areas is because once you commit to each other, there should be no problem submitting to this man and allowing him to lead your family into the happily ever after phase.

"Most successful men, because of their earning potential, will tend to look for women who are flexible in their career choices. What you do for a living or aspire to do will not be as important to him as who you are. I find this to be true with most men, but it is amplified with successful men."

Are You Sure You're Ready for A Baller

A financially successful man will obviously have the ability to provide a more comfortable lifestyle with many perks and amenities. However, with this extra gain comes extra risk. *"The higher the potential gain, the higher the risk,"* we say in the investment business. A successful man, because of his intense career focus, does everything to the tenth power. What he wants from a woman is the same, but he doesn't want to take forever to find out if she is capable of functioning at this level. Once you find out if he covers your 10 areas, you will have to jump right in and prove that you can provide all eight areas within two to four months before he moves on to someone else.

He tends to make decisions quickly and changes them slowly. Make sure you're ready to date a successful man who wants to be married because matrimony could happen in a year. If he thinks you're playing games, he will play you and think nothing of it. Because men who appear to be successful are approached all the time by women that are trying to get something from them. They have a very low tolerance for game of any nature; which is ironic because successful men sometimes tend to play the most games because of the constant attention they get from the opposite sex. Playing games gets old quick for successful men but getting women to take them serious once they are ready to settle down becomes their biggest challenge.

Most successful men, because of their earning potential, will tend to look for women who are flexible in their career choices. What you do for a living or aspire to do will not be as important to him as who you are. I find this to be true with most men, but it is amplified with successful men. Because their time is so limited, they tend to want you to make adjustments and be available for them. Traveling and relocation may all be possibilities with this type of man. So many women say they want a successful man until they begin to date one and realize that it is as much work as it is fun. Once you marry him, the fun part increases because you live together. That increases the time you can spend together and the resources you're able to use to make and keep him happy. Let me help you imagine the eight points I mentioned in the earlier paragraphs as they apply to the financially successful man.

1. A woman who is physically attractive to him may require her to be versatile in projecting her image in many different environments. He may require a woman who is universally attractive, someone who can demand the attention of an entire room, not just from him. Let me reiterate that this is a mindset you

must have. Charisma is sexy and goes a long way.

2. A woman who makes him feel like he is the love of her life.   This becomes even more important because he knows that he is going to expose you to men as equally wealthy and powerful as he may be, and perhaps more so. He must know beyond a shadow of doubt that he is the only one for you. You love him for him, not money because there is always someone else with more money.

3. A woman who makes him feel like she needs him mentally, emotionally, physically, and financially. The operative word is need. He cannot feel optional in your life. You know that you can achieve everything you want in your life on your own, and that's fine. Now keep it to yourself.

4. A woman who is fun to be around. This may require that you be more adventurous and learned. His status may have exposed him to many different things that require more involvement like areas such as golf, tennis,

and spontaneous travel to places like Las Vegas, California, New York, etc. He may be cultured and like things like art, wine, history, and languages. It's important that you take the time to find out what he likes. Be open-minded to try new things, but always be yourself. If you don't like something, say so.

5. A woman who understands the importance of food as a centerpiece around which to build family traditions of communication and love. Successful men tend to be non-traditional when it comes to food. They like to cross cultural lines and try more exotic things like sushi, caviar, and pâté, just to give a few examples. Don't be afraid to try new things and enjoy life. But never let go of your roots. He will always have a special place for the things his mother raised him on, so know how to cook old favorites.

6. A woman who is fabulous sexually. Please refer back to this one in the previous chapter because nothing has changed. For most men, the more successful they are, the higher the sex drive. He will be more of a breakfast,

lunch, and dinner type of lover. Don't be afraid to swing by the office for some midday loving on the desk, the floor, in the supply closet, or in the car.

7. A woman who is financially responsible. The more successful the man, the more important this point will become. For obvious reasons, he has a lot more to lose if he allows the wrong woman in his life. It could be the costliest mistake he will ever make. If he was counseled correctly, he believes a woman can either make you or break you. So finding the right mate is a critical decision that will probably be made more mentally than emotionally.

8. A woman who understands that a successful black man's love and obligation to his mother is a powerful force in his life. It will be very important to him that the two of you get along well. For this reason I stress even more that you make sure you love each other with all your hearts before you meet the family. They must feel you love each other or they will give you hell and assume you're a gold digger.

151

Listen, if you don't have your life together, don't date a successful man. His lifestyle will highlight areas of your life that are not together. Goals, vision, dreams, passion, focus, intensity, and time management, should be characteristics you see in a successful man and he will see them in you. You cannot fake these characteristics because they will manifest themselves in your life if you truly believe in yourself. This separates the doers from the talkers and perpetrators.

How to Meet and Date a Good Man

Let me start by saying that dating to find a wife or husband is not a game and it is not based on luck or prayer. It is a skill that can be achieved. Women of the 1940s and 1950s never doubted that they would find a husband. They were trained in the art of how to win a man's heart, and more than 60 % of them succeeded.

To date a good man, you must understand that he is not programmed for the dating game. Therefore, you cannot judge him by his performance in dating game situations. Some of the very characteristics that make him a good man also make him appear to be less aggressive in social environments. A good man should be confident, considerate, charismatic, charming, intelligent, and most of all, humble. All these characteristics are almost impossible to exercise and just as difficult to recognize by women in a club or social environment.

For instance, in today's clubs, men are yelling at women as they walk by, grabbing random body parts to solicit attention, approaching people's dinner tables, or interrupting conversations with friends or others to ask for a woman's name or phone number. Some women interpret these techniques as a display of confidence if the man is extremely attractive and rude if the man is average looking. The truth is that the techniques are arrogant and inconsiderate, no matter who does them, attractive or not. An intelligent and considerate man would never do them.

If you truly are interested in meeting a good man, you must first forget about all the rules you have heard about where to meet good men. Good men are everywhere and looking for the right women at all times. It does not matter if you're in church, the grocery store, the gym, gas station, or shopping mall. God places the right people in your path to achieve all your goals and dreams, but it's up to you to allow them into your life. What a good man would do is:

1. Attempt to make eye contact to find out if you're available and interested in him. (Ladies – when in public, attempt to make eye contact with people you find attractive until you find someone trying to make eye contact with you).

2. Then he will wait for an opportunity to talk to you alone to try to get to know you better and establish a method of communication in the future. (Ladies – when out with friends, make sure that a few times during the evening you make yourself available to be approached. Most women sit together, stand together,

dance together, go to the bathroom together, etc.

3. In a club environment he may ask you to dance first, allowing you both an opportunity to take a better look at each other to increase your physical attraction. However, he may offer to buy you a drink as a courtesy for the dance and a chance to talk to you further. (Ladies – don't demand that he buy you a drink. As a matter of fact, don't ask a good man for anything unless he asks you what you want).

4. He may not attempt to have a long conversation with you at the first meeting, understanding that you may have already had an agenda prior to meeting him. The second opportunity to talk feels so much more familiar and comfortable whether on the phone or in person on your first date.

Now as we move toward the first date, this is where the drama ensues because true intentions begin to manifest themselves in your actions. Courtship or dating as we call it was developed for one purpose, to find your mate. There are a lot of women who only date to get a free meal from a man or to get out of the house for an evening. I recall leaving a restaurant with a young lady and she gave her leftovers to a homeless person standing outside of the restaurant. When I asked her why she did so, she said food was free. My response was, "If I recall correctly, I had to pay the check before we left that restaurant." She had to laugh because she realized she slipped and let her true character show. This was a woman who had not paid for her own meal in so long that she thought food from restaurants was free, which for her, was true. It appears a lot of people date for fun and friendship. But please be sure if all you want is a friend, you make that perfectly clear before your first date.

The first date: a first date should have only one theme and that is to get to know each other. Don't allow this very important opportunity to be clouded by money or selfish motives to get someone to sponsor your entertainment agenda. If a man chooses the agenda for the first date, let him, as long as there will be a forum to get to know each other. If women set up the first date, choose something quaint not intimate like a coffee house or lunch at a moderately price café. Don't focus on what to order to eat, but on what is on his mind. Think of it as a race to get as much information about him as possible. The more you talk, the more you will learn about someone good or bad. Liars will box themselves into a corner and make it easy for you to find out what they are all about. Good men will enjoy opening up to someone who is attractive and interested in them. Successful men hate to waste time so maximize every moment in the beginning to get to know each other. You will have plenty of time to explore the pleasure of enjoying each other's company without saying a word if you have found the right person for you, but now is not the time. Technology has allowed us to make great strides in communication and yet we don't use these great advances to achieve our personal goals. Throughout your dating, the phone should be used as much as possible to talk to each other about as much as you can. Through the power of communication, you can turn a stranger into someone you feel you have known your entire life. This makes issues like intimacy and trust easier to adjust to.

The second date: the second date should be an intimate dinner in a very popular restaurant on the most crowded night. It can be a place that one or both of you have frequented before. This will give you some insight as to how this person lives his or her life. You may meet your date's friends and associates and if you're lucky you may run into other people this person may be dating or sleeping with. This is not to cause drama, but to make sure this person is not attached to someone else. See how the other person treats you in public. Do they respect you and keep you at the center of attention in the presence of other attractive people?

The third date: this date should take place at the home of the man. Either he can cook you dinner or order out, but you need to get into his environment as soon as possible. This allows you to see how he lives and match his words with his lifestyle. By the third date, you will know if he is married or has a live-in lover, whether he has a lot of traffic at his house, roommates, or how much his phone rings to get and idea of how much he dates. This will also provide insight into the life he will provide for you if you were to marry him someday. Now please be prepared on the next date to open your world to him just as he has to you. Remember that you want him to trust you as much as you want to trust him so make him want you.

If after dating for a month or two, you have decided this could be the person for you, than go for it. Understand the commitment to be exclusive must be mutual and verbal; there are no rules other than the ones you make together so design your relationship. Don't let fear of failing stop you from giving love a chance. If the chemistry between you is right and the other areas match in your lives, then give each other 100% and put the other person first.

What seems to be the most often asked question of people in relationships is, "How long should I wait for him to ask me to marry him?" Well, my standard answer has always been that if you feel it's been too long, then it has and you should move on. You don't want someone to marry you out of guilt or fear of loss. I believe a person knows if they love you and wants to spend the rest of their life with you from the time they lay eyes on you to a year, max. They should be prepared to make the commitment within 1 to 2 years. If you are in a relationship that has lasted more than 2 years and you're not engaged or married, it may be time to re-evaluate your relationship.

HOW TO DESTROY A RELATIONSHIP

Here is a quick list of things not to do:

A. Don't lie. You have no reason to. If someone can't love you for you, then move on. The truth always comes out.

B. Don't ask for money no matter how bad the situations you may be facing. Use the resources you already have to solve your financial problems. (Money is the cause of most relationships not working, so don't start off on the wrong path). Once a person has a chance to get to know you and care for you, there is nothing they won't do to help you. Give them that chance first.

C. Don't be jealous or over possessive. It's usually a sign of baggage from previous

159

relationships and would be considered offensive to a good man.

D. Don't pretend to be attracted to someone and continue to date him or her just to fill your social calendar if you know they are not your type. The most inconsiderate thing you can do to a good person is to waste their time and money.

E. Don't demand anything but respect and appreciate everything right down to a simple gesture of opening your door.

A group of women have settled into relationships with men they know are not right for them, but it provides them sex and companionship they need. It's convenient when they need it without interfering with their schedule. Most times, this type of behavior prevents the right person from coming into your life because it's already full of people, places and things. These dating practices continue to separate good black men from good black women. Let's talk about some other things to consider when it comes to dating.

Women, if you are honestly not ready to date, PLEASE stop dating. You're hurting good men and delaying the connection

process of the people who are ready for love. Yes, I know this goes both ways.

1) If you still have feelings for someone else in your past, stop dating.

2) If you are still bitter about your last break up, stop dating.

3) If you're not ready to be intimate with someone again, stop dating.

4) If you think all men are dogs and can't be trusted, stop dating.

5) If you currently have a man, but you're mad at him, stop dating.

6) If you put your career above having a relationship, stop dating.

7) If your life is not organized, (for example: child care or time in schedule), please stop dating.

8) If you're not looking for a relationship, stop dating. Just have friends who know that's all you want. Don't string men along.

9) If you're just looking for help with your bills, stop dating. Get a better job.

10) If you're looking for something to do because you're bored, stop dating. Read a book or get a hobby.

Ladies, do you want to know another reason so many men lie? Men lie because so many women date for the wrong reasons. Of the women I've spoken with, 99% of them believe, good men don't exist anyway. This attitude has men believing all women are playing games. As a result, a man's strategy is to only tell her what she wants to hear so she will have sex with him. It appears that only after sex do most women stop playing games. It's then when she let's you know what type of relationship she wants with you. The problem with lying as a technique to cut through the relationship games is that the truth eventually comes out. At that point, the possibility of trust is destroyed.

Men don't want to waste time or money dating a woman who has no intention of developing an emotionally or physically fulfilling relationship. Think, dinner at a moderate restaurant for two will cost approximately $55.00. Add a movie or the club and the cost goes up an additional $20 for a movie or $70.00 for the club with one drink each. That's $75.00 to $125.00 per date. If he dates twice a week it will cost $150.00 to $250.00 a week or $600 to $1000 a month if he dates every week. That does not include gifts, cards, flowers, Coach bags, etc. He could lease a Mercedes or pay the mortgage on a home in a nice neighborhood for that amount of money.

Based on what most men make, they simply cannot afford to date on a regular basis. They are continually making choices between paying bills and staying home alone, going into debt dating or lying to women to avoid spending money unnecessarily before you know if she is interested in a relationship or at the very least sex. Investing the money would not be so bad if everybody was being honest; a good wife is priceless. More often than not, nobody is being honest.

More and more women are saying they just want to develop a friendship first before they date someone. Well as you can see, friendship is very expensive for men, which is why most men won't agree to date as friends. However, there are a small percentage of men who will agree. But once again they're lying to get close to you in hopes that you will change your mind or feel sexually vulnerable one night. Those are the men who will be there to reap the benefits during your moment of weakness.

The concept of dating to become friends has proven to be nothing more than a scam to put men in a holding pattern so women can reap all the benefits of dating without the expectation of intimacy. So what he's taking you to dinner, movies, dancing, theater, concerts, etc. He's anticipating the time when he can graduate from friend zone to relationship zone. Now women know it's highly unlikely that will ever happen because single women don't put men they are physically attracted to or have sexual chemistry with on the friend program.

Let's be honest, the only difference between a friend and a boyfriend is chemistry and physical attraction. Some other important characteristics of a boyfriend are:

Trustworthiness - Worthy of your reliance on their integrity.

Loyal - Faithful to one's oath, engagements, or obligations.

Considerate - To be thoughtful, kind, understanding, and caring of another's feelings.

These are just a few of many characteristics we all look for in a mate. Now I agree that you should not have intercourse with someone whose character you don't feel comfortable with, but there are so many ways to show someone you're attracted to them and to let them know you feel chemistry without having sex. It's in the way you hold each other's hand, the way you look in each other's eyes, the way you kiss each other's lips, hands, forehead, eyelids, and neck. The way you hug, how long you hold on, the way you embrace when you meet and depart. If you spend the night together, do you spoon or sleep on opposite ends of the bed? Do you crave to feel that person's touch so much that if they get out the bed, his or her absence awakens you? You would be surprised how long a man will wait for sex if he feels and sees the obvious signs that show you genuinely care.

Let me share a story that was told to us:

> *Women need to stop playing games, as this one brother, Maurice puts it. If you're more interested in what a brother can do for you instead of what you can do for each other, don't date.*
>
> *Maurice had been single and dating for over a year when he ran into Monica. Monica was this gorgeous model who had recently moved with her roommate into the same luxury apartment Maurice lived in for the last two years. Maurice wanting to be in a relationship, so he began dating Monica with all the right intentions.*
>
> *Unfortunately, he experienced what thousands of good men experience all the time: just how manipulating and ruthless some women can be. Monica said all the right things in the beginning like, "I really want someone nice to be with. I want a man who knows how to treat a woman, etc." Maurice fell for her hook, line and sinker.*

Over the course of the next 2 months, she slept at his house four out of seven days a week. As a matter of fact, he gave her a key to his place because she didn't have furniture in her place yet to relax or watch TV. She was an aspiring model, so the jobs were sporadic. Maurice provided her with three square meals a day while at his house. She also did not have a car, so Maurice would take her to jobs, photo shoots, and pick her up no matter how late she would finish.

Now Maurice was fine with this because he really liked Monica and she said all the right things to keep him wanting to date her. Things like, "You're my baby. What did I do to deserve you? Just hang in there with me, and it will be worth it." As a matter of fact, he had a drawer full of little notes she would leave on his pillow expressing how he was everything she wanted. So here's a woman who's struggling financially that meets a man willing to get behind her and help her get on her feet. He wines and dines her, helps with her bills, spends time with her daughter and takes her out for her birthday, drives her to and from work, and allows her access to his home for her personal comfort.

There was only one problem as far as Maurice was concerned. Monica's actions did not match her words. Although she said he was everything she wanted in a man, had no problem putting it in writing everyday, had no problem excepting all the help she could get including a key to Maurice's house she used at least four to five days a week, she refused to be intimate with him at all other than a hug and a peck kiss on the lips. They slept in the same bed four plus nights a week with no sex or intimacy at all. She would tell him it was too soon, he needed to be patient, "Don't worry," she'd say, "it will happen when the time is right." Yet she felt the time was right for everything else he was doing for her. She got up from his bed, took a shower in his bathroom, cooked breakfast in his kitchen, and expected him to drive her to work that day.

A frustrated Maurice decided to confront Monica about her feelings and behavior toward him.
He sensed something wasn't right because her words and actions were not congruent. During a

heated conversation, Monica accused him of only wanting one thing; sex, after all he had done for her. Maurice had reached his tolerance level and asked Monica to gather her things and leave his key on the counter if she was not ready for a relationship. A pissed off Monica did not want to leave her gravy train and she lashed out, "Because I'm not fucking you, I'm not welcome here anymore?" Maurice firmly articulated that if this relationship was not going to be mutual, then she had to give up the benefits reserved for someone he would call his girlfriend. Instead of her defending the feelings she claimed to have for him, she called him every name in the book as he helped her get her stuff out his house. She phoned him the next day to express her disappointment with his decision even more, but her final words spoke volumes. She said, "That's okay. I'm on my way to have breakfast with the man I am fucking."

The fact of the matter is that Monica never cared about Maurice. She cared about what he represented to her, which was HELP. When you really care about someone, you want to please him as much as they want to please you. Now let me ask you, how many times do you think this expensive and heartbreaking scenario will be played out before Maurice, the good man, is good no more?

It's so important that we start to date honestly or we are going to cause irrevocable damage to male-female relationships.

"A man who has worked hard to be a good man, positioned himself to provide for a family, and has everything you're looking for should not have to earn your love or affection. He already has by being the man you said you wanted. He has been working his whole life for you, although he did not know you personally."

Playing Hard to Get Won't Get You Got

Some women believe playing hard to get will ultimately land them the man they desire. Wrong, dead wrong. Nothing could be further from the truth. From the time you meet a man, you already know if you'd like to get to know him better. Contrary to popular belief, men aren't as dumb as they act. We can tell if a woman is attracted to us and if she is not being true to those feelings while pretending to be disinterested. We also know all the reasons why women have philosophies like "I don't kiss on the first date." Or "I'm going to make him wait for at least three months before we have sex so I don't appear easy," and, "I like him but he is going to have to date me for a while. I hope he doesn't think sex is free. If you give him the milk, why should he buy the cow?" For the most part, if you play the hard to get game, it's not going to go like you think.

In case you haven't noticed from the previous chapters, men are very concerned with being misled or hurt by women. They will quickly turn into very insecure little boys when it comes to games. If they sense you're playing games, defenses will go up to avoid being vulnerable and hurt. Men may play along with you because they have decided to no longer have a relationship with you. They just want sex. Men then say what they need to say and pay what they need to pay to get you in bed. Once you have sex, you're now ready to pursue a serious relationship and they are ready to move on to someone else. Women immediately respond that men are dogs and only want one thing. It's the games women play that change a man's mindset from initially digging you to just screwing you.

The thrill of the chase now turns to fear and pain. People will do more to avoid pain than they will to gain pleasure. So now he's playing games and you start to sense something is wrong. A vicious cycle begins until someone decides to stop it. Something that could have been beautiful was extinguished before it had a chance to truly ignite.

The concept of playing hard to get actually came from women meeting men who were not up to their standards. Consequently, they made these men do things to improve themselves. If you are attracted to a nice guy with a good head on his shoulders but has an unstable career, I suggest you don't date him because he is not ready for a woman in his life. He needs to focus on his career, but you could tell him when he gets his act together to give you a call. This may give him the extra motivation to really do something with himself so he can have the women of his dreams. Now he may continue to pursue you, but don't give in until he has his act together. This is not playing hard to get. At this stage in his life, you are hard to get.

A man who has worked hard to be a good man, positioned himself to provide for a family, and has everything you're looking for should not have to earn your love or affection. He already has by being the man you said you wanted. He has been working his whole life for you, although he did not know you personally. After all the obstacles he has overcome from bad relationships to a society designed to destroy his passion for success or prosperity, he stands before you a good man with his act together. Now you want him to prove he deserves you? He is going to start wondering if you deserve him and will be insulted if you try to run game on him.

A man will never trust a woman who plays games. Don't get me wrong; a little mystery can be healthy. It gets the heart pumping. Curiosity is one of the greatest motivators. However, good men are also quick to quit and move on if they feel things aren't going their way. Good men don't have time to play games. If they see that's what is going on they'll be out of there faster than you can say, "Honey, I was only kidding". Two people who have chemistry trying to get to know each other nowadays are hard enough. Don't make it worse by playing and scheming. Men want to be around women who want to be around them. You'll have a better chance of landing a good man if you keep it real with him. So remember, playing hard to get won't get you got. It'll get you gone!

"Sometimes in our quest to make things better or easier, we compromise the very things that will allow our relationships to grow naturally to yield the result we seek. That is, to be happy and on the road to marriage."

No More Drama in Our Relationship

Let's talk about some of the decisions we make that cause us drama in our relationships. Sometimes in our quest to make things better or easier, we compromise the very things that will allow our relationships to grow naturally to yield the result we seek. That is, to be happy and on the road to marriage.

Don't be afraid of **time management** in your relationship. A lot of the time we have a fairy tale view of how dating should go. We want this spontaneous, romantic world-wind kind of relationship. I think you can have it, but you should have in place a foundation of time commitment to your relationship. Today, careers are so demanding that we tend to put so much time and energy into them and don't have much time for anything else. Having 24 hours to work with, if you work 9 hours including your commute, that leaves 15 hours left to live your life. If you sleep 8 hours that leaves 7 hours left to live the rest of your life everyday. In this time you must eat two or more meals a day, you must shit, shower, and shave at least once everyday, spend time with your children (if you have any), have personal time to unwind, workout, worship, and date that special someone. It is very important for you to have your life broken down into compartments like work, personal, family, worship and relationship. Each one of these areas won't get time on a daily basis, but I think it is dangerous for your sanity if they each don't get time on a weekly basis. Most people allow each area to dictate the time it needs. In other words, everything else competes for time based on demand except work. You visit your family or children when they demand it and you spend time with your boyfriend or girlfriend when they demand it. You go to church when your commitments demand it, you workout when your body demands it, you relax when your brain demands it, and you spend time with your friends when they demand it. The problem is that most of these things are demanding the same time periods in your life and you're being forced daily basis to juggle them while trying to make everyone happy including yourself.

This is where time management comes in. I believe you should have a date night already in your schedule every week and an additional day for the children to be included if you have any. Although not spontaneous, it can be quite romantic because it allows you to plan things without worrying if the other person is going to be available. It also gives you something to look forward to if the rest of the week gets busy and you don't get to see each other much. It prevents you from neglecting your relationship or your children as a major part of your week. Of course, if you can date more than one day a week, by all means do it. If you can spend more time as a family, do it. But if you're spending less time than one day in each area, you're not investing nearly enough time to nurture your relationships.

My advice to the men is if you are not planning something special for date night, do whatever she wants to do. Allow her to decide what she wants and likes to do. This will allow you to really get to know her interests and she can never complain that you don't do what pleases her. Also, do the same with the children. Get them involved with deciding what is going to happen on family night from games to dinner or a movie. This will give the children something to look forward to and a reason to be good all week.

On the days you don't see each other, make sure the last thing you do before you go to bed or before they go to bed is to speak with your significant other. Not only will this reinforce you're thinking about them and you care, but it also gives them peace of mind that you made it home safely and sleeping alone. Even for a very secure mate, this will unconsciously make them feel even more secure which gives them the extra comfort to commit when the time is right. Life is about the truth and the perception you give to each other. If you give the perception that your relationship is not important, it really won't matter if you love him or her more than life. The person in your life will eventually get tired of wondering if you care and leave or assume that you don't and retaliate. Perception is truly stronger than reality in every aspect of life. You must not only be honest, but you must make sure the perception you give matches reality. Don't allow the lack of time invested in your relationship to cause you drama.

In our attempt to simplify our time management issues and in some cases money issues, we make another potentially fatal decision. We decide to **live together** or as some call it, have a **trial marriage**. I have heard so many arguments for living together as a way to see if you're right for each other. But when you get right down to it 90% of the time the decision is more about money than love. The man, woman, or both see an opportunity to save money. I think most women do believe they've got him if they live with him. They think that living together is truly one step away from marriage.

Marriage is two people becoming one flesh, living in harmony. This is the single most emotionally expensive decision you will ever make. Getting married is like building a huge house; you not only must consider the cost of building the house but also the cost of maintaining it as well. You see, it's not just making the commitment but maintaining the commitment for the rest of your life. It's not something that should be entered into lightly. If you're not sure you're ready the last thing you should do is live with someone.

You must change your life to incorporate someone else in every major decision you make. This will probably be the hardest thing you will ever do in your life. The only thing that makes it easier and even possible is the commitment. Two people living together without a commitment is really stacking the odds against them that the relationship will grow naturally to the next step of marriage.

Most people think that love is the key to making the living arrangement work or that having no expectations except to save money will somehow make things easier. None of this is true. I've had roommates early in my life. And no matter how well we got along as friends, living together was always tough. These relationships are difficult to share your personal space 24 hours a day. They lack a commitment to make it work no matter what.

You see, if you're still getting to know each other, you need your space to evaluate the progress of the relationship and decide if this is the person for you without feeling trapped. And if you feel that you, why can't you just get married? I don't want to hear the excuses of saving money for the wedding because it doesn't cost more than $100 in most states to get married. You can always have a wedding later when you can afford it.

I bet a lot of people are saying they know couples that have lived together and now they are married. I don't doubt that. Many couples end up marrying after years of living together and having children. Men who are not planning to leave home to be with another woman will surrender to marriage so as not to lose the security of home life. Most men who get married after living with someone do so out of a feeling of surrender. In some cases, they have actually been given a choice to either step up make the commitment or step off.

I believe one of the reasons the divorce rate is so high amongst African Americans is because many men are forced to get married. Also, many women are marrying to fulfill a dream of having a wedding instead of a lifetime commitment to become one flesh with the person they have promised their life to before God.

This brings me to my next point of keeping the drama out of your relationship. **Do not become dependent in any way on the money of another person who is not your spouse**. In other words, do not buy a car together, house together, credit cards together, furniture together, investments together, cell phones together, etc. There should be no monetary exchanges of any kind between you and someone you're dating other than gifts. If it is not a gift you don't mind them taking if the relationship goes sour, then don't give it to them.

Money has not only been the cause of many marriages failing, but is also the reason countless relationships don't last. When people invest money in you other than a gift, they expect a return on their investment. Your relationship has now turned into a business deal instead of a loving and naturally progressing courtship. You're now making decisions based on whether the other person will get angry, get your car repossessed or put you out the house when they should be based on love and commitment. Today there are many people dating just to find someone to pay their bills. This would be fine if you fall in love and marry the person first. So remember, give presents you feel the person deserves without the expectation of a return.

Women, if you ever intend to have a serious relationship with the potential for marriage, don't ask a man for anything financial. Just allow him to give to you what he wants. That will allow you to see what type of man you're dealing with. When you ask a man you barely know for money, he begins to feel that money must be the reason you're with him. He may play along and give you the money, but he will not look at you as a candidate for marriage. You become a woman he has an arrangement with, sex for money.

Another area that causes so much drama in your relationships is what we call **baby mama or baby daddy drama**. This drama occurs between people with children from previous relationships. They refuse to let the relationship with the parent of their child or children go. Instead of focusing on their relationship with the children, they complicate the life of a former partner. Harassing an ex makes more since to them than moving on and having a healthy and drama free future with someone else. So, they maintain the drama to make their ex miserable.

People who share children should only have to communicate about child-related issues such as visitation arrangements, financial obligations, disciplinary policies, and educational decisions. None of these decisions need to be discussed late at night or early in the morning. None of it really needs to be discussed in person. If you want to avoid unnecessary drama, make sure you have all the arrangements documented and signed in the presence of a notary public. If you're in a serious relationship and your ex is causing drama, you can show your significant other the notarized arrangements. This will clarify to your current partner the level of involvement between you and your ex. This will reduce the amount that personal feeling for each other is involved in making decisions about the children, just follow the arrangements or get a court order. Until you decide to get married, there is no reason why your ex-companion should communicate with your current companion other than to be cordial if they speak over the phone or upon meeting. If you're dating someone with children, try to avoid any involvement with the other parent until you truly love the one you're with. And if you interact with the children, be a friend. Leave the parenting to the parents. Your relationship and role in the children's lives will grow naturally as your role changes in their parent's life.

Next is, **don't take advice from anyone who has not been where you want to go.** We tend to get all our dating advice from our single, bitter friends who have never been married. They want to protect you so they only focus on the negative things that can happen. It's difficult enough to date and set aside prejudices from prior relationships. Now you're carrying the prejudices of all your friends and family members from their bad relationships. They never tell you what role they may have played in the demise of their past debacles. All they tell you are the negative things their mate did and how yours is probably the same way.

Also, whether it's conscious or unconscious, jealousy and envy exist between most close friends and family members. If they feel you slipping away from them to spend more time with that new significant other in your life, they really don't like it and will fight to keep you close to them.

An area of your relationships that seems to cause so much drama is **sex and cheating**. Sex is not a gift; it is a lifestyle choice. Once you choose a sexual lifestyle, you must be careful about the changes you make and be sure you can handle all the consequences that may accompany the changes. Make sure you are sexually compatible before you enter a committed relationship with someone. Afterwards, don't change unless you both agree to change. If you choose to be celibate, that's great. Only date celibate people or you're increasing the chances of someone being unfaithful to you.

If both of you are sexually active at the time you start the relationship, you should not decide to become celibate in the middle of the relationship unless the other person agrees to do the same. If not, you're forcing someone to change his or her lifestyle. When that happens, look forward to acts of infidelity and/or the end of your relationship. If you're a male who likes to have threesomes, then date a woman who is into that as well. Don't try to convince women to try it for your birthday or as a gift for a special occasion.

Convincing your mate to participate in a sexual act, which involves other people can be emotionally damaging and cause extreme insecurity in your relationship. I don't think one night of interesting sex is worth destroying a relationship with someone you love. For bisexual women, please make sure your boyfriend consents to you having female sexual partners before you commit to a monogamous relationship. Cheating is cheating whether it is with the same sex or not unless you make clear the ambiguity beforehand.

I hear a lot of women ask, "Why do men cheat? Well I'll attempt to give you another answer. As you can see by now, there are multiple reasons why we have some of the problems in our relationships. Lying and cheating happens for so many reasons and I try to explore as many of them as I can in this book. When it comes to cheating, I always say that you can't shoot someone if the gun is not loaded. A man can't cheat with an empty weapon, so ladies empty the weapon every chance you get. I don't think I need to go into detail as to the many ways you can empty the weapon. Truth be told men really don't care what method you use. As you may know, there are very few men who are multi-orgasmic. Most men max at three a day unlike women who are multi-orgasmic and can have many more than three, potentially creating a voracious sexual appetite. But what scares men most is women don't have to be stimulated to have sex as often and with as many partners in a day as she wants. Let's face it, most women claim not to orgasm in most of their sexual encounters with men anyway.

The desire to orgasm is what usually fuels a person's sexual appetite. Some men do have a very high sexual appetite and it is up to you to find out what your man's appetite is. Some men like their sex like their food; for breakfast, lunch, and dinner. You need to empty the weapon in the morning, preferably before he uses the bathroom, stop by his job or entice him to come home for lunch time love making, and finish him off for dessert before he goes to bed. Other men may like it twice a day or once a day or once a week. Whatever your man's appetite is, find it and satisfy it. You will significantly reduce the chance of your man cheating. Men, you must find a woman with high moral standards and make her happy in every area of life. You then significantly reduce the chance of her cheating. If you find your sexual appetites don't match, maybe he or she is not the right person for you. Move on and find someone with which you're equally matched.

Another reason men have affairs is because every time he sees his lover or mistress, he knows beyond a shadow of doubt they are going to have sex. Sex is what their relationship is based on and what he can count on. He's sure about what he's getting from his mistress but isn't sure of what to expect from his girlfriend or wife. Too many married men or men in monogamous relationships have no clue when the next time they are going to have any type of sexual contact with their mates. You see, if the mistress has a headache or just isn't in the mood, she won't meet with him leaving him available to explore other options of getting sex elsewhere. If the wife or girlfriend is not in the mood or has a headache, she still expects him to come home or to her house. And you better not have an attitude or she accuses you of only wanting one thing. He may not know what you're going to do intimately, but he should know that you're going to do something the next time he sees you. You can get too comfortable in a relationship and forget to do little things like hug and kiss, to acknowledge you missed each other while you were apart.

I do realize that the sex drive of the human male is unhealthy. As stated in <u>The Physiological Value of Continence</u>, by Dr. R.W. Bernard, A.B., M.A., PH.D. "Man is sexually perverted. He is the only animal that has this social problem, the only animal that supports prostitution, the only animal that practices self-abuse, the only animal that is demoralized by all forms of sexual perversions the only animal whose male will attack the females, the only animal where the desire of the female is not the law, the only one that does not exercise his sexual powers in harmony with their primitive constitution."

It went on to further state that "civilized man practices copulation all the time, and in most cases without intention to conceive while so-called savages and primitive races leading more natural lives and who follow their natural instincts to a greater extent are far chaste in their sexual behavior." This has led to the conclusion that the sex life of civilized men is unnatural. "The excessive manifestation of the sex urge among them is due to a feeling of confinement and certain aphrodisiacal stimuli rather than to natural instinct. Among such stimuli are a high-protein meat diet (accompanied by physical inactivity), the use of tobacco, alcohol and coffee, sexually stimulating literature, dramas, motion pictures, conversation, etc."

When I read this I realized how they keep us focused on sex and use it to keep us as consumers unable to focus on living right. If we are going to be successful in relationships or anything else, we must control our exposure to such stimuli. Women, if you want to help your man, you must first marry him before you provide a home environment to bring him closer to the way our creator intended he live. So match his sexual lifestyle first. Once you're married, promote a healthier lifestyle by controlling your family's diet and over-exposure to sexual stimuli.

The Aftermath

What keeps a good man and a good woman from exposing their hearts? The number one reason is rejection for men and trust for women. Many women may argue, "Well, we get rejected also." This may be true, and just as many men have a problem with trust. However, it's nowhere near the degree that men face rejection or women have trust issues. Now I'm going to explain why good women have to get back in the dating world and with a new attitude, or should I say an old attitude.

Most of the time in dating, women are pursued. The good women go straight home from work, don't go out to clubs or restaurants, and don't date men at the job or church. Every time a man approaches you, the answer is no because you're not looking for love. You're waiting for love to happen. The rest of the time he is out approaching women who look him up and down to see how much money he has. If she can't see it in the diamonds in his ear or on his wrist, she looks to see what type of rims are on his car. If he has none of the above, the answer is no.

I have been fairly successful in my life and I have always driven a nice car, but I never believed in jewelry or diamonds. I always thought you bought them for your wife not yourself. I've never been one to wear trendy cloths with visible designer labels.

Because I have always been in a traditional industry such as financial services, I have had to look good but conservative.

It amazes me how little attention I get when standing in a club or restaurant as opposed to the women who follow me in my car, write their numbers on a piece of paper and throw it through my window at the light. Some have approached my car and asked, "Why are you all alone? Can I ride with you? My point is I'm treated like a rock star when I'm driving in my car and invisible when I'm not. This is a rampant misconception of women in our community because the real women are not dating anymore.

I've heard some woman say, "I'm out all the time but men just don't approach me." The question is, are you approachable? Most women have a very unapproachable look and don't flirt very much anymore. I assume this may be the result of being bombarded by undesirable men. You must learn to target your flirtation and encourage good men to risk rejection and humiliation by approaching you. Rejection equals pain and pain equals change, so good men have stopped approaching women who don't give them a sign that she wants to be approached. It's mental conditioning, which is a very powerful technique for controlling behavior. Whether it's done intentionally or not it is very effective. Like an elephant at the circus, we've all seen this massive, 2000+lbs creature restrained by a small rope around its ankle. How can this be? Surely the elephant is stronger than 100

190

men and could break free anytime it chooses, right? Wrong! The elephant doesn't believe it can break free because as a baby elephant a massive chain discouraged its movement. When the small elephant tried to break lose, it failed. It was denied and rejected over and over again. When something is tied around its ankle as an adult, it remembers the rejection and failure of past attempts to escape. From a chain to a small rope fastened around the elephant's ankle, it will no longer attempt to escape. Psychological conditioning has done that. Are many good women guilty of this type of mental programming because they just didn't want to be bothered?

Think about how many times a man has spoken to you and you didn't speak back? How many times has a man smiled at you, only for you to act as if he didn't exist? How many times have you been at a party dancing against the wall, but when a brother asks you if you want to dance with him it's, "No thank you," but you'll dance all night with your girlfriend who came to the club with you. It doesn't hurt you to speak to someone and it doesn't kill you to dance with someone even if they aren't your types. A good man will observe you to see if you're with anyone or if you appear to want to be bothered. If you appear to be rejecting people randomly without making any attempt to get to know anyone, he will avoid approaching you. Smart men only take calculated risks. Idiots will follow each other off a cliff. So when you have them lined up waiting to say something to you, who do you think is in that line?

Time is like money and good men don't like to waste either. Encourage conversation with people if you're single. You never know if Mr. Right is watching to see if he should approach you. Being attractive is like being famous to a certain degree. There are benefits and drawbacks. In both cases, you get a lot of attention wherever you go. Sometimes you like it and sometimes you don't feel like being bothered. But just like the famous person, you have to be nice or get out of the public eye. If you're not in a good mood, stay home. We have witnessed this scene time and time again. A brother set out across the room to a group of women standing by themselves only to return moments later humiliated and rejected. Very rarely have we ever seen a woman speak to a man and he didn't speak back or ask him to dance and he wouldn't dance with her even if he thought she was not his type.

Everyone has a flashing sign on their chest that says, "make me feel good," Men particularly, have embraced that sentiment and go out of their way, to make women feel good. A lot of times women are down right rude! No one likes to be rejected and just because we're men, it doesn't mean we don't have feelings.

Men understand that women expect them to do things to show their appreciation for her love and support. They should. A man will only take care of the woman he loves and believes loves him. He feels it whenever she is around. Everything else is game and only game. How many of you know women who are very attractive and have dated all the athletes and entertainers and players? Yet today they are single with nothing to show for it. They don't own a home or if they do, they have a mortgage they struggle to pay every month. The designer cloths are out of style or don't fit anymore, they have pawned the jewelry or lost it and are bouncing from man to man to make ends meet.

Your 20s are just 10 short years. I assure you that for most of you, the decisions you make during those years will have the biggest effect on your dating philosophy than the rest of your years combined. If you don't think the Hip-Hop culture is influencing the way we date and how we treat each other, just listen to the music. "Ball till you fall," is what they use to sing about! "Will you still love me if I fall off," and "I think she wants me for my pimp juice," is what they are singing now. It's obvious the Hip-Hop culture is here to stay, but let's not let it be at the price of black love. We can have them both if we don't let entertainment dictate our reality. We must consciously create our own reality, black men and women together.

"If I could only dream one dream
Or have one wish come true
It would be for you to marry me
To hear you say, "I DO"
I heard Black Love was dead
But we're about to prove them wrong
Forty years from now, they'll be saying
I knew they'd make it all along."

MARRY ME

Do you remember when I first stepped to you?
And asked you for your name
You gave me that evil look that said
Return from whence you came
And brother could you please refrain
From spittin' any of your lame game
Even though I wasn't to blame
For the last guy that caused you so much pain
You held it against me
And my advances were in vain.
Thank God, I didn't listen
Thank God I could see
That you were my soulmate
Not who you were pretending to be.
That's why it gives me great pleasure
To grab your hand and take a knee
I want to spend the rest of my life with you
Will you please marry me?

We can have a wonderful life
We can build a happy home
We can work together
Instead of trying to do it on our own.
Don't listen to all the fiction
Baby, that's what's caused all the friction
We're surrounded by contradiction.
They say Black men won't commit
But as you can see
That's absolutely not true
I am well aware that my world revolves around you.
For years, people have prophesized the demise
Of all the good black guys

Saying, we don't give a damn
About the tears in our sista's eyes.
Well, I'm a man who understands
That it was you who came from my rib
It's you who'll bear 9 hours of labor
Just to have my kids
Me, take you for granted
I never will, God forbid
I'm proposing with a ring
That's what I did
Thank God I didn't listen
Thank God I could see
That I was meant for you and you for me
That's why it gives me great pleasure
To grab your hand and take a knee
I want to spend the rest of my life with you
Will you please marry me?

For you I'd break my back
Work my fingers until they bleed
Fall asleep suffocating my pain every night
To give you what you need.
When I wanted someone I could count on
I decided to ask my heart
Its answer was what I knew it would be
With you was a great place to start.
Your beauty, your values
How much you show you care
I'm blessed to have a partner
Who is truly beyond compare.
When I was in trouble
It was you who came to my aid
When my so-called friends left my side
You were the one who stayed.
When I was sick and out of work

It was the money that you lent
That helped a brother stay afloat
And afford to pay his rent.
That's why I know true love exists
I can testify that it's not just a cliché'
Good men and women can find each other
It happened to us one day.
Thank God I didn't listen
Thank God I could see
That you and I were written in the stars
It was our destiny
That's why it gives me great pleasure
To grab your hand and take a knee
I want to spend the rest of my life with you
Will you please marry me?

If I could only dream one dream
Or have one wish come true
It would be for you to marry me
To hear you say, "I DO"
I heard Black Love was dead
But we're about to prove them wrong
Forty years from now, they'll be saying
I knew they'd make it all along.
So baby, don't doubt what you feel
You know our love is for real
I understand what you've been through
And I won't betray your trust
I promise it will never be just about me
It will always be about us.
Through good and bad times I'll adore you
Through thick and thin I'll stay
How I treat you the day of our wedding
Is how I'll treat you each and everyday.
My sacrifice, my commitment and my love

This I give to you for free
All I ask in return
Is will you please marry me?
My knee is getting weak
And my hands are getting sweaty
So will you hurry up?
And say yes Already

By Aaron Blake

IV. WILL YOU MARRY ME?

This is the question a man asks a woman when he is ready to provide for her mental, physical, emotional, and financial needs for the rest of his life. Yes, is the answer a woman gives when she agrees to provide for his mental, physical, and emotional needs until her death. If we all take a little time to pick the right person, marriage is the most beautiful relationship in the world. A person chooses to love you as they love themselves, unconditionally and without prejudice. So why do so few of us aspire to this level of love? Men are saying, "Women fall in two categories: far too independent or far too dependent." Women are saying, "What do I need a man for? And all men lie and cheat." When I hear these responses I hear issues of independence, power, money, and trust. These are the symptoms of a disease called fear. The fear of being dependent on someone or being vulnerable might allow someone to disappoint or hurt you. What if they do hurt you? In a couple of months to a year you will be just fine. But what if they don't hurt you and truly fall in love with you with every fiber in their bodies? You will experience the life God intended for you and happiness at a level only a great marriage can give.

We Need Each Other, Believe it or Not

In 1960, three-quarters of African American children were born to married couples. I can go back even further to say that only 18% of black women married in the 1940s were eventually divorced. This statistic is slightly higher than their white counterparts. Currently, marriage rates are down and divorce and childbirth out of wedlock are increasing rapidly for everyone. But the negative changes have been the greatest for African Americans. For example, in 1950s the percentage of married white women and black women were about the same, 67 % and 64 % respectively. By 1998, the rate dropped 13 % to 58 % for white women, and dropped 44 % to 36 % for black women.

Today it just gets worst for black women. 29 % aged 15 and over were married with their spouse present in the home, compared to 55 % of White women and 49 % of Hispanic women. I say this to point out that there is no coincidence as to why we have the most social problems of any other ethnic group. African Americans make up 12 % of the population, yet we have the lowest marriage rate, highest divorce rate, largest birth rate out of wedlock, the highest prison occupancy, highest rate of death from AIDS, lowest academic test scores, lowest participation in college prep courses, etc.

While black women spend their money trying to raise children alone and keep up with the Jones', black men are spending their money trying to impress and date women while maintaining separate households. If we continue at this pace, we will cease to exist in the future. Most of you may find this inconceivable. I suggest you study history of civilizations that no longer exist to find out who they were, the size of their population, and what caused them end. I think you will find groups larger than ours that have disappeared from society.

We need each other to maintain affordable housing. We need each other to provide adequate parenting to our children. We need each other to decrease promiscuous behavior and decrease the spread of AIDS in our community. We need each other to pool our resources and increase our economic and political strength. We need each other's love and support to build a community that nurtures and protect our children. We need each other to lower our frivolous spending and free up more money to save toward retirement, college education, and estate planning to leave an inheritance to our children's children. We need each other to increase the titles of wife, mother, husband, and father; and lower the number of bitches, hoes, prostitutes, players and pimps. We need each other so we can spend less time dating and more time living our lives in a way that honors God.

Let's also look at the emotional benefits. When that special someone loves us, cares for us, respects us, appreciates us and genuinely likes us unconditionally, it's the best feeling in the world. Having that special someone to celebrate your successes and that shoulder to cry during our darkest moments is a fundamental need of every human being. Now remember, I said that special someone. Yes, we can get all of the things I mentioned earlier from a variety of different people in a variety of different ways. However, it will always have more meaning when it comes from your mate.

Because of love and the feelings it brings, I still pursue women even though I'm sometimes afraid. Afraid of being vulnerable, rejected, abandoned, afraid of trusting, and of being hurt. Fear can immobilize love. It's not until you do what you fear the most that the death of fear is certain. Complaining and blaming each other has gotten us nowhere. When challenges occur, both partners are usually responsible because both of you are trying to prevent being hurt or disappointed.

Are You Living by God's or Man's Plan

The problem with creating a successful relationship in this country is there is no set of guidelines as to how to live your life. Although America is supposed to be a melting pot, African Americans seem to be the only ones melting. Freedom is one of the greatest things about living in America; it is also the biggest problem we have with establishing a lifestyle to build a relationship and a community. The Constitution allows us the freedom of religion or lack thereof. It also separates church from state. So what you have is a constant struggle between how our choice of religion says we should live and what capitalism has designed as a lifestyle for us.

If you study Mesopotamian and Egyptian civilizations, the oldest advanced cultures in the world, you will find that there was no separation of government and religion. Whoever was in charge of the government was also in control of the culture's religion or spiritual beliefs. Every decision made by government was in harmony with religion or religion was changed to bring about harmony.

The focus of the people was to live in harmony with the beliefs of the leadership, thought to be from God or the closest to god on earth. This mindset and style of leadership has continued in many cultures for centuries and still exists today in many countries. Whether we agree with their lifestyles or not, they have less social problems with marriage, relationships, and childbirth than we do. It seems that poverty and war has created most of the social problems of the world. The reason for poverty seems to be corruption in governments and war seems to be based on religious factions fighting for control over government. In simplest terms, this is what the Middle East troubles are all about Jews, Palestinians, and Muslims fighting for land, leadership, and money.

When Constantine came to power as the first Christian Emperor of Rome, he planned to unify government and religion. He found that the largest part of Rome consisted of Pagans. Jews were the largest single religion and Christians were the new but fast growing faction. Christians were considered a threat and were fighting persecution. So Constantine brokered a compromise between Christians and Pagans because neither group was organized with concrete doctrine. This agreement would make him a very powerful leader controlling the masses. The Christians were taught by word of mouth passed down for generations since the death of Jesus Christ. The Pagans' worshiped many different gods for many reasons, but nothing was in writing to give them direction. The Jewish religion, having been established for thousands of years with written laws and commandments, would require the Roman Empire to change too much. Jews were wealthy and strong in numbers. Furthermore, they had the Ten Commandments and the Torah, which consist of the first five books of the Bible. Once all the writings of the prophets were brought together to form the Bible and Pagans were allowed to still celebrate their holidays, which some correlating with religious beliefs, all of Rome became Christians or Jews. They named the church the Roman Catholic Church, meaning the universal church of God. The first Pope was appointed and soon the church had power over the masses. The church influenced the life of the people and government controlled the army while the Emperor controlled them both. About 600 years later the formation of Islam by the Prophet Muhammad and the growth of Judaism and Christianity made it more difficult for one religious group to rule over the others. As government continued its pursuit of money and power, its views continued to separate from the teachings of the church causing conflict. This was the foundation of our philosophy on separation of church and state.

Eventually laws were passed separating church and state. Of course, this made the state more powerful. We live under the same type of system today. We also live in a capitalist society, which allows everyone to pursue wealth and power, not just the government. This has caused three agendas to develop. First, you have the government that wants everyone to work and pay taxes so it can continue to be the most powerful military protecting the most powerful country in the world.

Then you have corporations that want to exploit our labor for as little money as possible, while encouraging us to spend every dime we earn trying to maintain a lifestyle we can't possibly afford. They offer us credit to make things appear manageable until it's too late and you're in debt over your head. This makes you more dependent on the corporations and takes away your ability to negotiate a fair salary for the work you do in fear of losing your job.

Finally, you have the church that has adapted to today's capitalist mindset, which is to make as much money as possible. It encourages you to work, prosper, and tithe, while allowing more and more deviations from the true teachings of the Bible to help people adjust to the three agendas in this country. If the church is telling you that you must tithe to prosper, and the government is requiring you to pay taxes to live in this country, and corporations pay to little for labor and charge too much for goods and services, forcing you to go into debt to survive. It's a wonder we can make since of anything in our lives right now.

This has caused our priorities to change. Instead of religion being our way of life, capitalism is now our way of life, and the government extorts money for protecting our freedoms. Now success is not judged by whether you're a good servant of God, good husband or wife and father or mother. Success is now based on how much money you make and spend and power is based on how much money you contribute to the political process. They have used the media to control our thoughts and keep us focused on capitalism as our way of life and only after you have achieved financial and material success should you began to focus on marriage, children, and God.

Everyone who studies the numbers knows that only the top 5% of this country make it to a level of financial independence, and the number is closer to 1% become financially independent in the African American community. Most African Americans are making financial success their number one priority. Very few will ever become financial independent because of poor career choices, deplorable saving habits, and no investment knowledge while spending most of their life pursuing a goal they have no chance of achieving. What gets neglected are love, relationship, marriage and children - true representations of success and family. They provide the foundation to build a financially prosperous lifestyle.

God wants you to serve Him and provide for your wife. Women help your men and teach your children. Society wants you to pursue money and spend it all on goods and services while forgetting about family and community. This plan affects our community the most because we have no forces working against it. Most ethnic groups have a strong culture to pass down traditions like religion, marriage, children, and financial success in that order.

White America has various cultures and traditions it passes from generation to generation. Regardless of the particular European ethnicity, the importance of religion, marriage, children and financial success are stressed respectively. Most African Americans have no culture or traditions that lead to happiness or financial independence anymore. We don't even think like a community anymore. We are a bunch of individuals trying to make money so we can integrate into someone else's culture. Every man or woman for themselves and by any means necessary, irrespective of future consequences to our children and their children, is the mindset the majority of our people are displaying.

The most powerful and successful people in this country don't try to hide how they became that way anymore. They show us what they have and how they got it, but not how they keep it. The reason why they don't show us how they keep it is because the answer to that question is personal. Family is the key. When you build a strong family as the foundation for wealth creation, you not only achieve wealth faster, but also can pass that wealth from one generation to the next with each generation increasing the wealth, not squandering it. Corporate CEOs can earn hundreds of millions of dollars a year in salaries and stock options, and amass fortunes worth billions, and political connections that are priceless. Most of them did not do this overnight. It took generations of wealth and powerful connections to get to those positions. Other cultures don't worry about African Americans becoming strong political or business contenders because that would require wealth to last more than one generation. It would also require the wealthy families in the African American community to work together toward a common goal. Sounds simple enough, but there's only one problem. We can't come together as man and woman to form a family.

As long as we stay single, we purchase twice as many homes or rent twice as many apartments, spend twice as much on food, twice as much on utilities and phones, and twice as much on entertainment because single people go out more trying to meet each other. We will always be consumers instead of entrepreneurs and investors.

There was a time when we would be happy with a modest home we owned, a simple car for transportation, simple meals on our tables, and clothes on our families' backs. Now we need very expensive homes with rooms we don't use, luxury cars with all the latest gadgets, gourmet food, and designer clothes. Our children are watching us fight to obtain this material gain we can't afford and they desire it for themselves.

In America, children born after 1964 referred to as Generation X because nobody knows what is going to happen to them in the job market. They are expected to be the first generation to do worst than their parents financially. And it's only getting worse. We don't have the same opportunities our parents had, so our young men are selling drugs and our young women are selling their bodies to live like ghetto superstars. Ask yourself, am I going to live as God intended and prioritize building a family and a strong community to serve and glorify him, or am I going to neglect the future and just live for today spending all my time making and spending money glorifying designer labels? No one can slave for two masters, for either he will hate the one and love the other, or he will stick to the one and despise the other. You cannot slave for God and for riches. (Matthew 6:24) If you live by God's plan, riches will come and whether you've done what is right with your riches will be for God to judge.

Marriage is The Answer

Are you ready for marriage? In case you vow a vow to your God, you must not be slow about paying it, because your God will without fail require it of you, and it would indeed become a sin on your part. (Deuteronomy 23:21) Who so find a wife find a good thing, and obtain favour of the Lord. (Proverbs 18:22)

As you see, marriage is a big decision that should not be entered into lightly. You should really be sure you're ready to give unselfishly to the building of a successful family unit. Therefore shall a man leave his father and his mother, and shall cleave unto his wife: and they shall be one flesh. (Genesis 2:24)

A vital factor to this is the ability to make a wholehearted commitment. This all starts with personal preparation. Are your characteristics that of fruit of the Spirit, which is love, joy, peace, longsuffering, gentleness, goodness, faith, mildness and self – controlled? (Galatians 5:22, 23)

Women, when a man is deciding to marry, your heart is more important than your physical appearance. Be modest and of sound mind to enhance your wisdom, which is true beauty. Men be kind, respectful, make decisions and be responsible while being modest and humble. These are characteristics you should be working to improve before you ever meet and fall in love with someone. Once you're in a relationship they are a must to be successful.

The burden of dating correctly to find a mate is largely the responsibility of the women and the responsibility of headship puts the burden of marriage on men. If done correctly, the courtship should last no more than 2 years. The marriage should last the rest of your life. So women, it is worth it for you to take the lead, and hold to your standards, and don't play games when dating.

The next step is to open your heart and let love in. I can imagine some of you are scared of commitment, especially after understanding how serious it is to make a commitment to marry before God. But that is why love is so important. There is no fear in love; but perfect love cast out fear: because fear exercises a restraint. He that is under fear has not been made perfect in love. (1 John 4:18)

As we go through life with goals to achieve great things as individuals, we forget about the importance of love. I don't mean the love of your family, friends and God, but the love of your neighbor, a spouse, and your enemy. If I speak in the tongues of men and of angels but do not have love, I have become a sounding brass or a clashing cymbal. And if I have the gift of prophesying and am acquainted with all the sacred secrets and all knowledge, and if I have all the faith so as to transplant mountains but do not have love, I am nothing. And if I give all my belongings to feed others and if I hand over my body, that I may boast, but do not have love, I am not profited at all. Love is long–suffering and kind. Love is not jealous it does not brag does not get puffed up. It does not behave indecently, does not look for its own interests, and does not become provoked. It does not keep account of the injury. It does not rejoice over unrighteousness, but rejoices with the truth. It bears all things, believes all things, hopes all things, and endures all things. (1 Corinthians 13: 1- 7)

After reading this I hope some of you truthfully admit that you have never known love before. Yet, you avoid it like the plague and blame it for all the heartbreak you suffered in past relationships.

What is a family? It's the oldest institution and the foundation of some of the strongest societies. The family has taken many forms throughout civilization. I think we have all types of families in the African American community. The traditional family involves a father, mother, and siblings and is the best way to raise children to maturity. Sure, a single parent can succeed at raising children, but it will be difficult on the parent and the child. Aaron and I are products of single parent homes raised solely by our mothers. I think we came out okay, but it was difficult. You also have extended families living in the same household, including one or both grandparents. Many cultures view this method as the best way to raise a child. I'm sure there are great cases for and against each alternative to traditional households.

Unfortunately, we don't always have a choice of what type of environment our children are raised, but we must always fight for the best possible situation. Family is a haven of safety and security for children who look to their parents for emotional and physical support. Family is also the place were women are queens; she is loved and adored by the husband at her head and the children at her feet. Both of them looking for her approval and support day after day.

Secrets of a successful marriage and family life

1) Love each other
2) Respect each other
3) Have Christ-like Headship
4) Wifely Subjection
5) Good communication, speak lightly
6) Live within your means, debt equals stress
7) Encourage each other, don't criticize
8) Train your children on discipline and respect
9) Share the load of managing a household
10) Keep God at the center of your family

I don't claim to be an expert at marriage, but I do know what made my marriage last over seven years and I know what caused us problems. If you make sure you're compatible before you get married and practice these ten principles after you're married, the odds are on your side that you will have a great marriage.

"If black women stop having children out of wedlock, our population would fail to reproduce itself and would rapidly die off. Married black women are having on average less than 0.9 children per marriage." *"I read that a black child born during the time of slavery was more likely to grow up living with both parents than he or she is today."*

Selfishness May Equal Self-destruction

The attitude that persists today about there being no good men or no good women has got to stop. This attitude is very destructive. Not only that, it becomes a self-fulfilling prophecy. What you believe becomes reality. Whether you think there are or you think there aren't good people out there, it manifests in your life.

We can't keep neglecting each other and think it's without consequence. Lets look at some very startling facts. If black women stop having children out of wedlock, our population would fail to reproduce itself and would rapidly die off. Married black women are having on average less than 0.9 children per marriage. I read that a black child born during the time of slavery was more likely to grow up living with both parents than he or she is today. Only one-third of African American children has two parents in the home. It's said that an African American girl exposed to single motherhood at some point during her adolescent years has a 100 % chance of becoming a single mother.

Now is the time for us to embrace one another, to share in the responsibility for where we are and work together to bring about a change. By any means necessary we must heal the wounds between black men and black women. First and foremost, we must believe in each other again. We must believe we can make love work and once again be committed to each other. When you love someone, you work on solutions. We want to love you and we want you to love us back. To experience this bond, we must be open and vulnerable to each other. Yes, that exposes us to some pain. However, love is the most powerful force in the universe. This tenet I hold true and will endure the pain one more time until I get it right. I truly believe it's better to love temporarily than to suffer life without love permanently.

So many sisters are giving up on good men because they've had unpleasant experiences with a bad man. I thought trials and tribulations were supposed to make you better, not make you quit. They should help even if they hurt you. Currently many of you are postponing your happiness, living your life with regrets, and walking past good men everyday. I'm calling on both, men and women alike, to reclaim what is rightfully ours; happy, loving relationships. Let's agree that we will no longer let our relationships fall by the wayside because we're afraid. Let's proclaim that we do need each other. It's essential to our survival. We have grown to far apart and it's time to reconnect.

To many men and women have chosen to remain single and some have even chosen to not have children. This concerns me so dearly because every other culture in history has ever question whether a man or woman should marry and have children. The first thing God did after creating Eve was to tell her and Adam to be fruitful and multiply. If your objective is to live your life in a way that is pleasing to God, how does remaining single or choosing to be childless but remaining sexually active for pleasure achieve that objective? I'm aware that being single can be a gift when the kingdom of the heavens ordains it. If you have chosen to give your life entirely to serve and not be married or bear children for a Godly purpose, then bless you. But if your decision is purely selfish to avoid the responsibility of a committed relationship while enjoying the benefits of dating, then you are our biggest problem.

Independence is an overrated experience. It's just led to single parent homes, children without their fathers, poverty running rampant, jealousy among each other, manipulation and distrust, not to mention sexual exploitation, and the breakdown of our spiritual foundation. That's all it's done to us!

Let's all make a commitment to change for the better, open our hearts to the right person, and begin a relationship that upholds the foundation of our ancestry and community. Why not build a legacy of love, family and wealth to leave to our children!

219

"Now is the time for us to embrace one another, to share in the responsibility for where we are and work together to bring about a change. By any means necessary we must heal the wounds between black men and black women."

Notes

1. Annual Demographic Survey from The Bureau of Labor Statistics and The Bureau of the Census revised March 2002,

2. Data for 2000 from The Bureau of Labor Statistics and The Bureau of the Census revised March 2002, Marital Status

3. Bureau of the Census, Marital Status and Living arrangements: March 2002,

4. The Physiological Value of Continence, by Dr. R.W. Bernard, A.B., M.A., PH.D.

5. New World Translation of the Holy Scriptures, rendered from the original languages, revised 1984

6. The King James Version of the Bible, Old and New testament, and New International Version, 1997

7. The Abolition of Marriage, by Maggie Gallagher p 117, citing Andrew J. Cherlin, Marriage, Divorce, Remarriage, rev. and enl. Ed., (Cambridge, Mass.: Harvard University Press, 1992), 98-99

8. Data for 1950 from Bureau of the Census, Census of the Population: 1950, vol.1, General Population Characteristics (Washington, D.C.: U.S. Government Printing Office, 1952),

ABOUT THE AUTHORS

We are the Jekyle and Hyde of love and relationships. We had one lifestyle that became two very different lifestyles as the result of a chemical reaction called love, just as Dr. Jekyle, one man became two very different people as a result of a chemical reaction. We were both raised in single parent homes headed by women who helped each other try to keep the two of us in line from a very young age. Aaron's father was near by and did participate in his life, while my father choose not to participate in my life at all after age 7. This may have resulted in Aaron becoming a great student and an athlete, while I ignored school and focused on the streets, dancing, rapping, and experimenting with everything bad, what you call a thug today. Yet we were inseparable most of our childhood one influencing the other good and bad.

By high school I straightened up my life just enough to get into college, while Aaron was an honor role student an all state athlete with a choice of Universities he could attend. It seemed like we were back on the same page with goals to go to college and become engineers. Then like a chemical reaction we seem to have switched lives. I went on to excel at everything I touched which should have been expected of Aaron, while Aaron's success has come through a lot of turmoil and strife in the area of career and relationships which should have been expected of me based upon my track record. What happened to change the direction of these two men's lives? Women! They have been the primary influence in what type of men we were and now are.

In high school I began to date women from neighboring schools that had successful parents and were excellent students and had goals to attend some of the most prestigious universities in the country, who would rather die than disappoint their parents or themselves. I began to do everything in my power to live up to the expectations of the women I was dating and gain the acceptance of their parents. This also made me value just how hard my mother worked to provide for me and how proud she would be If I did something great with my life. Aaron met his first true love at 16 years old she was older than he was, with her own apartment and a 2-year-old son she had dropped out of high school to raise by herself. He began to do what she expected of him to make her happy, which was far less than what he had planned for his life.

I left for college following the women in my life while Aaron left for college with the woman he loved at home pregnant with his child, and a young son to raise. I continued to pursue my career got married and worked on living a comfortable lifestyle while Aaron returned home to raise a family in the hood. What happened to us from then to now is what gives us both a unique view on love and relationship which is reflected in this book for everyone to learn what they might from our journey to find love and happiness.

Women acknowledge the power you have to shape the life of the men that love you just by your expectations, love and support. Men respect and value the strength of our women who bring balance and purpose to our lives, that we may reach our God given potential to lead and love all things as God leads and loves us. Thank you, and may we all find love and happiness in the very near future.

Author's Biography

Christopher J. Cokley was born in Newark NJ, educated in the Asbury Park, N.J. School system. He attended KEAN University in N.J., was a recipient of the Mary and William Burch Scholarship for Academics and Community Service, and awarded undergraduate Omega Man of the Year, for leadership by Omega Psi Phi Fraternity, Inc.

As well he held the position of President of the Townsend Lecture Series, responsible in part for the funding and hospitality of lecturers brought in by student organizations. He also held the position of Resident Advisor for three years, responsible for monitoring and aiding freshman adjustment in coed dormitories all year including summer programs.

He took an independent contractor position with a financial service marketing company his senior year of college. Within six months he was promoted to Regional Vice President. In two years, he was promoted for the seventh time to National Sales Director at 23 years old. At the time, it was the top position in the company reporting to the CEO of the largest financial service marketing company in the world. Chris has been involved with the recruitment, training, development and mentoring of thousands of couples and individuals throughout his 16-year, career with the same company in the finance industry. It was his enormous exposure and interaction with so many different people that has given Chris his unique insight on love, life and relationships. He now resides in Atlanta, GA.

Author's Biography

Aaron Maurice Blake was born Dec. 9th 1967 in Neptune, N.J. He graduated from Asbury Park High School with Honors. He accepted an academic scholarship to attend New Jersey Institute of Technology in Newark, N.J. He then went to work with a very large financial services marketing company. There he was one of the top regional managers in the country. He helped to train and develop hundreds of other company leaders and won numerous awards. He has specialized in mortgages for the last several years. Today, he is a very successful mortgage consultant residing in Atlanta, GA.

Printed in the United States
15791LVS00001B/172-231